Am I Dead Yet?

Am I Dead Yet?

71 Countries, 36 War Zones, One Man's Opinion

John Scully

Fitzhenry & Whiteside

Fitzhenry and Whiteside Limited
195 Allstate Parkway, Markham, Ontario L3R 4T8

In the United States:
311 Washington Street, Brighton, Massachusetts 02135

www.fitzhenry.ca   godwit@fitzhenry.ca

Fitzhenry & Whiteside acknowledges with thanks the Canada Council for the Arts, and the Ontario Arts Council for their support of our publishing program. We acknowledge the financial support of the Government of Canada through the Book Publishing Industry Development Program (BPIDP) for our publishing activities.

Library and Archives Canada Cataloguing in Publication
Scully, John
Am I dead yet? / John Scully.
ISBN 978-1-55455-090-6
1. Scully, John. 2. Terrorism. 3. Imperialism. 4. War correspondents—Canada—Biography. 5. Foreign correspondents—Canada—Biography. 6. Television journalists—Canada—Biography. I. Title.
PN4913.S38A3 2008   070.4'333092   C2008-900066-8

United States Cataloguing-in-Publication Data
Scully, John.
Am I dead yet? / John Scully.
Originally published: CN: Indigo Premier Plus, 2007
[240] p. : cm.
Summary: The career of this awarding-winning television journalist, including his trips to seventy countries to create news stories and documentaries for the BBC and CBC.
ISBN-13: 9781554550906
1. Scully, John. 2. War correspondents—Canada—Biography. 3. Foreign correspondents—Canada—Biography. 4. Television journalists—Canada—Biography I. Title.
070.4/333092 dc22   PN4913.S38Am 2008

Cover design by David Drummond
Cover image courtesy John Scully
Interior design by Karen Petherick Thomas
Printed and bound in Canada

1 3 5 7 9 10 8 6 4 2

ENVIRONMENTAL BENEFITS STATEMENT

Fitzhenry & Whiteside saved the following resources by printing the pages of this book on chlorine free paper made with 100% post-consumer waste.

TREES	WATER	ENERGY	SOLID WASTE	GREENHOUSE GASES
42	15,313	29	1,966	3,689
FULLY GROWN	GALLONS	MILLION BTUs	POUNDS	POUNDS

Calculations based on research by Environmental Defense and the Paper Task Force.
Manufactured at Friesens Corporation

Contents

Prologue

This is the book I promised I would never write. I have been a journalist for fifty years. I have covered stories in seventy countries. I have worked for the very best and the very worst international broadcasters. So I must have learned something, right? What I've learned is that "war stories" can be deadly boring. Or they can be brilliant. I decided long ago not to take the risk and make myself look like a fool by writing a boring book. So I didn't. Then came my grandson, Liam. So I changed my mind in case he was ever curious about what I did. Oh, so Scully's just a silly, old softie and not the grumpy, old asshole we all think he is?

Well, that's not the only reason. What I see happening now in Iraq and other parts of the Middle East drives me nuts. Doesn't anyone read history anymore? Doesn't anyone see parallels between now and the very recent past? And why are we so appalled by massacres and ethnic cleansing in the Balkans, that we send in squadrons of NATO bombers but ignore the genocides of Rwanda and Darfur? Well, er, um, you see, how can I put it? They're not white!

Enough ranting, already. But the book is not boring, I promise. It is sometimes sad, even tragic, but often very silly. It uses the "F" word too much and displays an unhealthy obsession with certain bodily functions. Children should be accompanied at all times as I take you on my own journeys of discovery and realization. I hope that you will find them, well, brilliant. I feel a Nobel Prize coming on. No. Whew! That's just the meds kicking in.

1

Spot the Terrorist

"Al-Qaeda are cowards!"
"The IRA are cowards!"
"Hezbollah are cowards!"

Hmm. The refrain sounds familiar. I first heard it from a South Vietnamese general: "The Viet Cong are bloody cowards! They won't stand and fight."

No, they wouldn't and that's why they won the war. The "bloody cowards" had massed no more than a kilometer away, just beyond the tree line and were about to launch their final offensive to take Saigon. Not bad for a bunch of skinny men and women in black pajamas.

The war had cost them a million lives or thereabouts. Yet they humiliated the world's most powerful military force—outfoxed them, outwitted them, killed when they weren't supposed to and fought from secret hideouts and tunnels deep underground. They had the support through terror or belief of the local villagers (plus help from Russia and China) who saw tens of thousands of foreign killers on a mission from God, well from the U.S.: stop Communism (or any ideology or religion the U.S. did not like) from spreading like falling dominoes or the States might be next.

They believed it then, and now, and have learned nothing.

The lessons of Vietnam and other conflicts have been ignored. For example, in one of its more recent invasions of southern Lebanon, the brilliant, brutal Israeli military thought it could use the U.S. saturation bombing tactics against Hezbollah, who, like the Viet Cong, are highly organized, locally supported (with help from Syria and Iran), and operate out of tunnels deep underground. The bombs killed civilians, flattened buildings but did not flatten Hezbollah.

On this April day in 1975, the humbled U.S., South Koreans, Aussies and a few Kiwis had long gone. Putting up an impenetrable wall of defense now was one solitary tank of the Army of the Republic of Vietnam (the "good guys"). It loosed off a few desultory rounds in the direction of the tree line to manic shrieks of applause from the tank crew and a few remaining soldiers who, curiously, had not fled to the woods themselves. Maybe it was payday.

Suddenly, a helicopter buzzed the tank trench. It was the general, obviously in need of intense psychiatric intervention, trying to get the VC to give away their positions by firing at him. No chance. They were having too much fun watching, although, as a goodwill gesture, their mortars incinerated two press cars. The general replied by unleashing a pod of rockets from his chopper, just missing two of his own men and three gentlemen of the Canadian press corps, Mr. Walter Corbett, Mr. Peter Trueman and Mr. John Scully. Then, mercifully, he landed.

"That'll show the bloody cowards! You. You Canada, you come with me, I show you just what cowards the VC are."

"Huh?"

"You fly with me. I show you VC."

"Ah, thanks, general, but we've got to get back to file our stories."

"No problem. I fly you to Saigon later."

"Well, we've got a van here with all our equipment."

"Okay. I'll bring you right back here. You are here to cover a war, so come with me."

"But where are we going?"

"To see the VC!"

Oh, shit. As combat virgins we thought this was perhaps the way you really did cover a war.

"Get in before Charlie shoots us!"

"Who's Charlie?"

"Charlie! The VC!"

Again, oh, shit.

Up we clattered, with the demented general chuckling as he wheeled his chopper toward tree line at a height of about thirty meters.

"There! There! You see them? They too scared to shoot. I go lower."

No shots from the Viet Cong whom we could see darting around the tree line.

"Too scared. Bloody cowards."

It didn't occur to him that the VC just didn't care and didn't want to waste bullets on a nutbar.

Two weeks later they took Saigon … and the mad general.

In its last dying days Saigon was chaos. Refugees teemed into the city ahead of the unstoppable North Vietnamese who, for three decades, had been fueled with utter dedication to drive out the invaders and their surrogates, a willingness to die in their thousands and the belief in ultimate and total victory by any means necessary.

Throughout the Vietnam War, many in the United States and the media labeled the Viet Cong "terrorists." Were they? Before we go back to explore the effects of the Vietnam War, let us have a look at that word *terrorist* itself. Is it the correct noun to apply to insurgents, guerrillas, rebels or freedom fighters since all have employed the same tactics for centuries to defeat predators and marauders and to bring justice to the oppressed? The word terrorist is often used lazily and inaccurately. Terrorists are driven by sheer criminality, causeless brutality, greed, bravado, ignorance and woefully misunderstood religious teachings. They are seldom inspired by ideology, sound theology or history.

And when does a terrorist become a freedom fighter? South Africa and its supporters branded Nelson Mandela a terrorist. They jailed him because he led the African National Congress and supported its violent armed struggle to overthrow the apartheid regimes that had oppressed black South Africans for decades. Now Mandela is a world symbol of peace and reconciliation. However, there is an argument that some of his successors are terrorists but in a very different way from the Viet Cong or Mandela. President Thabo Mbeki has denied HIV causes AIDS while five-and-a-half million South Africans are infected and the epidemic has not yet peaked. Mbeki's health minister advocated the use of traditional medicines like garlic and lemon instead of antiretroviral drugs. The government has been internationally accused of adopting "lunatic fringe" attitudes of ignorance and denial toward HIV/AIDS. Meanwhile, more than five hundred

South Africans die every day. Every six days, the number of dead surpasses the total of those killed on the "terrorist attacks" of September 11. That would make Mbeki's government responsible for tens of thousands of the deaths because of their hubris and ignorance. To me, that makes them terrorists.

And what do you now call Menachem Begin, former Prime Minister of Israel? In the early 1940s he led the violent Irgun insurgents who killed and maimed in a quest to form a Jewish home and to drive the British and the Palestinians out. It culminated with the bombing of the King David Hotel in Jerusalem in which ninety-one people died: British, Jews and Arabs. Later, as a Nobel Peace Prize laureate, Begin wrote: "The revolt sprang from the earth ... A new generation grew up which turned its back on fear. It began to fight instead of to plead." A fairly classic definition of a freedom fighter. To Jews, he is a hero, to Arabs, a terrorist.

The Viet Cong were, like the Irgun, fighting for a homeland and driving out foreign armies. So, just whom can one justifiably label a terrorist? In South America, the only plausible reason for members of the Revolutionary Armed Forces of Colombia— known by its Spanish acronym simply as FARC—to kill, kidnap and terrorize fellow Colombians is to control the drug trade. Another Colombian group, the AUC, the United Self-Defense Forces of Colombia, is a paramilitary gang of thugs largely armed and funded by the government (with a lot of help from the U.S.) to kill its opponents—peasants, clergy, union workers, mothers and other "threats to democracy." FARC are terrorists. The AUC are terrorists. The allegedly police-supported death squads who are killing hundreds of noisome street kids because they are blots on the landscapes of Honduras, Guatemala and Brazil are terrorists, as are the Latino gangs, *Mara Salvatrucha,* of El Salvador who terrorize for money and control. They all kill for nothing else but money and muscle.

And that brings us to today's most abused phrases, "Muslim terrorists," "Islamic fundamentalists," "Muslim extremists." The latest repository of all knowledge, true and false, Wikipedia, describes the Chechens who precipitated the Beslan school massacre in which nearly two hundred Russian school kids and one hundred and fifty civilians died, as "Muslim terrorists." Here comes that lazy-phrase feeling again. Context is always a drag for both encyclopediacs and journalists. Context takes a long time to tell and gets in the way of fast, breaking facts. The writer may have been dissuaded from using quick, political shorthand if he or she had thought about the fact Chechens have been trying to subdue Russian domination since the eighteenth century; or that in 1944 the Russians massacred thousands of Chechens and deported the remaining population to Siberia where a quarter of a million died as refugees. Stalin's spurious excuse was that the Chechens might help Hitler defeat Russia in World War II. Whenever there is a so-called "terrorist" act, think back. Can one ever excuse the massacre of a hundred and fifty school kids? Of course not. Perhaps the more important question is: Do we understand why it happened? And what will prevent it happening again? Beslan had a lot to do with history and politics and precious little with "Muslim terrorism."

We'll look more at terrorism as my own journey around the world continues. First let's go back and see what happened in Vietnam and see why it still matters today.

Vietnam had precious little to do with religion, except that mainly Christian Westerners were fighting a country of Communist heathens. Eighty percent of Vietnamese say they don't practice any religion; those who do are mainly Buddhist and Roman Catholic. At the end of the war, though, many were doing a lot of praying, especially those who would be judged complicit with the U.S. One of the refugees I met was from the old Imperial capital of Hue where four thousand civilians died as the city was blasted to rubble. She was a university student, slim, very pretty, aged about twenty. She told me the Viet Cong would kill her because her family had been friends with the Americans—in what way, she didn't reveal. Her mum may have been a translator, a secretary or an informer. All she would tell me is that she had to escape Vietnam but she didn't have any money to get to the southern coast where an epic twentieth-century exodus had begun. Tens of thousands of boat people were escaping in rickety, rusting old fishing hulks, rafts, rowboats, anything their money could buy. Some found eventual, relative safety on the beaches of Thailand, Malaysia, the Philippines, Indonesia and even Australia. Others found rape and death at the hands of Thai pirates, or death by starvation, thirst and disease, or by drowning in furious, terrifying seas.

As the waves flung a never-ending tide of Vietnamese onto the beaches, patience, mercy and money began to run dry in the air-conditioned offices of governments in Southeast Asia. The Malaysians decided they could not handle any more refugees from a war that had nothing to do with them and threatened to force any more back out to sea. Was this just tough talk they hoped would be heard back in Vietnam and force the boat people to try to land somewhere else? We decided to find out as part of a CTV (Canadian Television) documentary we were making on the boat people.

We headed for one of the beaches where two packed boats had reportedly landed during the night. And then we saw them: a queue of about sixty dazed and broken refugees being herded on to two buses by gun-waving Malaysian soldiers. Where were they going? Would they really be forced back out to sea where others in their two boats had starved and died or were washed overboard and eaten by sharks?

We soon had our answers. We stopped our car about twenty meters ahead of the buses and Randy Platt began filming, until a soldier saw him, whipped his rifle in to the firing position and took aim. Randy got the message and lowered his camera. We drove away. The Malaysians did not want anyone, least of all a Western TV crew, to witness what would amount to premeditated murder.

A couple of kilometers from the buses, a local fisherman showed us a hiding place high above an inlet and then he scurried away. Through the bushes, the telephoto lens saw two old, battered boats with Vietnamese markings. Two Malaysian tugboats had attached lines to them. They were going to tow the boat people back out to sea and cut them adrift.

The morning was warm, humid and windy and the sea was running high as the buses pulled in to a jetty at the top of the inlet. Meekly, submissively, it seemed, the Vietnamese got back in their boats. No, they would not cause any more trouble.

The tugs pulled them from the jetty and away from the land, away from Malaysia into the churning sea, to the edge of the horizon. And then they were gone. That surely is an act of terrorism.

Those who had been lucky enough to be given refuge by Malaysia were taken to the tiny island of Pulao Bidong where several thousand were held in slime and their own filth. Engineers, lawyers, doctors, teenagers, mothers, babies. A sixteen-year-old girl described how Thai pirates stopped her boat and slit the throats of her father and two other men.

"Then they took turns at raping me in front of my mother. There were six of them. They raped me. They raped me. They raped me," was all she could say in a glassy-eyed monotone. A UN worker said several girls had already committed suicide and wondered if this one would be next.

The pretty student from Hue knew of the horrors of the boat people, but was still determined to escape.

"Two dollars, that's all I will charge."

She swore she had never been a prostitute until now.

"One dollar. One dollar. I come to your room. I good. One dollar."

One good old Yankee dollar. The good old Yankees had gone. Fifty-eight thousand of them had died but their legacy lived on.

Wonder if she made it.

⇥ ● ⇤

The Vietnam War was tragic, sad and pathetic just like any war. But the Vietnam War has a knack of never ending. Take a trip to the Washington memorial for the U.S. dead that twenty-one-year-old Maya Ying Lin, an Ohio architect of Chinese descent, designed. And wouldn't you know, there was outrage that a good old Yankee was not chosen to design the monument. It is a massive slab of black granite with the name of every man and every woman killed. And every day, men with paunches, men with gray pony tails, men in suits still raise their hands in aching grief as their fingers caress the names of their dead buddies. There you will see old moms and pops still leaden in death, still not done mourning their dead son or daughter. And young adults frown deeply as they wonder who their father was apart from a name carved in that black granite that bends and arcs as if trying to envelop the sorrowful, trying to tell them, it's okay, it's okay.

But it's not okay and the Vietnam War never ends, not in Washington where it all began. Only now it's called the "war on terrorism." No one's come right out and said it but it's also the war on Muslims. War is the way to go, in Washington, London and other complicit countries.

2

Have You Told Them About Jonestown?

Five years after the United States pulled out of Vietnam, there was another apocalyptical tragedy that appeared unconnected to the war. It was called Jonestown, in Guyana, in northeastern South America. Nine hundred disciples of cultist Jim Jones took cyanide in Flavor Aid and died before the world could act on reports of brutalities in Jones's Peoples Temple. Earlier in the day, on the nearby airstrip, Jones and his guards shot dead four men who had flown in to investigate: U.S. congressman Leo Ryan and three journalists: Don Harris and Robert Brown of NBC, and Greg Robinson of the *San Francisco Examiner*. They also murdered defector Patricia Parks.

Several years later, in 1982, I stood on that airstrip with a crew from CTV's current affairs program, *W-Five*. We had flown in to film Jonestown because it was to be resurrected in a bizarre scheme that had been hatched in Charlotte, North Carolina, and in a refugee camp in northern Thailand. The refugee camp was on a rocky hillside rutted with steep alleys and mud roads. It was the new home of the Hmong (pronounced "mong").

The Hmong are an ancient people, descendents of hunters from indigenous settlements in the frozen north, possibly Siberia or Mongolia. They number about ten million and their homelands now are the mountain regions of China, Thailand, Burma, North Vietnam and Laos. And it was the Laotian Hmong to whom the U.S. turned for help in the Vietnam War. A straight-faced United States publicly vowed to respect the neutrality of Laos; but the North Vietnamese supply line, the Ho Chi Minh trail, ran through the mountains of Laos into Vietnam. The United States could send only bombers, not troops, to block the supplies and to fight the Pathet Lao, a guerrilla movement closely allied to the Viet Cong, and who were also fighting the U.S.-backed Royal Lao Army. So the CIA orchestrated a "secret war" against the Pathet Lao, and they recruited the Hmong as its foot soldiers. The CIA conned the Hmong into believing the Vietnamese planned to take Hmong land and the U.S. would help defend them. So the Hmong fought; they guided U.S. bombing sorties and they rescued hundreds of shot-down pilots.

When Washington was done with them and left defeated and demoralized, it left the Hmong and the rest of its former partners to fend for themselves. Many were slaughtered by the victorious Pathet Lao who vowed to purge the Hmong from their country. It's estimated seventeen thousand Hmong soldiers died in the secret war in which the enemy used not only heavy weapons but also what the Hmong describe as "a yellow rain," possibly chem-ical and biological weapons. Thirty thousand civilians also died. It is alleged that many of those who stayed behind in 1975 were tortured and murdered. Some Hmong today claim Laos has launched a campaign of racial genocide against them. But one hundred thousand Hmong did manage to flee to Thailand and its fetid refugee camps.

Help—of a kind—was coming, at least for the Hmong in

Thailand. And who was this good Samaritan? The jut-jawed Christian evangelist who has condemned Islam as "evil," the son of Billy, the one, the only, Franklin Graham, head of the messianic, self-laudatory "Samaritan's Purse." First, Franklin and the men and women with divine guidance from Jesus Christ Almighty and the U.S. government chose Denver as the best place in the Lord's whole, wide, glorious world to settle the few hundred Hmong Uncle Sam decided he could tolerate. The problem was, the Hmong could not tolerate Denver and this strange city in this strange land of concrete and big bellies where something called snow nearly froze them to death in a season called winter. They lived in Spartan, armylike house-rows, ate inedible Western food and wanted to go home. They knew that was impossible, so they started killing themselves.

So what did the Christians do? They prayed.

"And please, Lord, guide our television crew that they may take good pictures and have a successful day. Amen."

In 1978, I spent two weeks with Franklin and a busload of his missionaries in sweltering northern Thailand. I survived their insouciance, their giddy God-praising, their hubris and their right-eousness by adopting a few guerrilla tactics of my own: Since they had banned alcohol I made a point of finding a cold beer in every village where we stopped. But just in case they took serious offense and tossed me out, or even worse, prayed for me, I tried always to breathe through my nose, despite a massive head cold, in case they smelled the evil liquid. I made a vow never to say "fuck" and, most important, never to take the Lord's name in vain.

In the refugee camp, there was Franklin telling the Hmong about this lovely jungle he knew in far-off Guyana. It was neat!

It had buildings, and birds and animals, and all that stuff. Tell you what! Come back with us and we'll show you!

"Okay."

"Have you told them about Jonestown?" I asked Franklin.

"Yes, but it doesn't seem to bother them."

Huh?

I doubt Franklin knew it, but the Hmong are traditional animists who believe in the spirit world—but surprise, surprise, many have now converted to Christianity.

In Guyana's capital, Georgetown, there was a motley zoo with a few birds, a couple of monkeys and not a lot else. That's where the missionaries, and their evangelical host, attorney Sir Lionel Luckhoo, nicknamed "the Perry Mason of the Caribbean," first took the unsuspecting Hmong party of four leaders. The Hmong were not dressed in their own colorful, indigenous clothes but were buttoned down in new dark trousers, shiny black shoes and short-sleeved shirts. They looked all set to go door-knocking for Jesus. The zoo was supposed to represent all the wonderful mountain wildlife Guyana had to offer. The Hmong didn't have much to say and didn't ask many questions, so it was off to Jonestown in a small chartered plane. We were told there wasn't enough room for us four from CTV. However, the missionaries wanted the photo-op, but a controlled one without pesky questions and nosy lenses, so they brought along their own film crew from Chicago and, of course, we could use their footage.

Not so fast, sunshine. We chartered our own plane for the hour-long flight up to Matthew's Ridge, the landing strip next to the tin huts that were Jonestown. But, what a shock—the government refused us permission to fly that day, but we could

go tomorrow. Samaritan's Purse and the lads had Guyana by the …
Well, let's say they and Sir Lionel were brothers in God and it was
God's will that we would not accompany them.

· A few hours later, back came the chosen few and the Hmong.

"So what happened up there?"

"Well, the Hmong seemed very impressed with the facilities.
They had a good, hard look."

"So they're going to settle in Jonestown?"

"They haven't said so. They want to go back and discuss it
with their people in Thailand. But, you know, wouldn't it be wonderful if Jonestown could rise from the ashes and be resurrected
for the good of man in the name of the Lord?"

Wonderful, except that when we landed at Matthew's Ridge
the next day, the local cop refused to let us leave the airstrip.
Censored again. Why? Probably Jonestown was not the Club
Med Franklin had implied, and probably Guyana's government
had had enough of foreigners poking at a still-festering wound.

And the Hmong? They never came back. Jonestown was just
too creepy. And, oh yeah, the Hmong believe the souls of the
deceased will come back to their ancestors for reincarnation.
Wouldn't want that to happen in Jonestown, would you?

Note: The U.S. began accepting more and more Hmong
refugees as memories dimmed. Now they number around two
hundred thousand.

3

Banana Terrorism

Franklin Graham's condemnation of Islam came in the hours and days after the attacks of September 11. Here's one for the record book: "The god of Islam is not the same God of the Christian or the Judeo-Christian faith. It is a different god, and I believe a very evil and a very wicked religion."

Three days later he said: "Let's use the weapons we have, the weapons of mass destruction if need be and destroy the enemy." But then Franklin had second thoughts after being condemned as a war-mongering racist. He wrote on his website: "Some of my recent statements, interpreted as critical of Islam, have been widely reported. I believe I've been greatly misunderstood." Not really. I think the world understood perfectly what he was saying and he proved unable to resist expressing his true feelings further down in the same Web article: "The Koran provides ample evidence that Islam encourages violence in order to win converts and to reach the ultimate goal of an Islamic world." The Koran does no such thing but Franklin is not a theological giant; sadly, nor are most of the seventy million U.S. Christian evangelicals who listen to him and others, like the influential millionaire televangelist Pat Robertson, who called for the assassination of Venezuelan President Hugo Chavez because he was building "a launching pad for Muslim extremists." Both men propagate hatred, but as Christian men of God they are allowed to spout their extremist venom without fear of arrest or recrimination while similar vitriol earns Muslim clerics arrest and deportation for hate crimes. Both Graham (and his dad) and Robertson are devout followers of the two Presidents Bush; Franklin even said the prayer at the younger Bush's inauguration.

The outbursts were an expression of shock, not just at the loss of life on 9/11 but also that the country's security had been invaded. Well, then, there's a twist. Let's look just a little to the south where we'll find a dozen countries that have been militarily and diplomatically invaded by the U.S. with a cost to life incomparably more awesome than the mere three thousand who died in the World Trade Center, the Pentagon and in Pennsylvania. If they weren't so poor and did not have Saudi money backing them, the perpetrators of 9/11 might just as easily have come from those countries, who still bear the wounds and the hatred toward a nation that bullied, killed and acted as if it had the right to go wherever its might and money could take it. The more impoverished the country, with hidden treasures of bananas, coffee, sugar, oil, minerals and cheap, cheap labor, the better. Countries such as Cuba, Mexico, Haiti, Honduras, the Dominican Republic, Panama, Colombia, Guatemala, Nicaragua and El Salvador.

The U.S. commercial muscle came from Mamita Unay or Mummy United but the local workers had little affection for the United Fruit Company of America that exploited and dominated the banana industry in Central America for eighty years. All of this has had a lasting economic impact and has entrenched American influence in the region to this day. However, some countries finally appear to have found a way to hit back: elections run free of intimidation, free from U.S. influence and bribery that have resulted in anti-U.S. governments run not by puppets but by indigenous leaders or fervent nationalists. Their determination to diminish U.S. imperialism has a great parallel in the events of September 11.

⇥ ● ⇤

We all remember where we were when we first heard about the attacks. September 11, 2001, began as a sunny Toronto morning, the temperature a comfortable 16°C. Around 8:30, I strolled the two blocks from the Holiday Inn on King Street to the CBC's Broadcast Centre to prepare for a day I would spend training regional TV reporters. A couple of keeners were already in the cavernous studio that was our home for a week. By our scheduled start time, nine o'clock, we were still waiting for a few stragglers. A couple of minutes later, a goggle-eyed reporter, Geoff Leo, arrived. "Have you guys heard? I've just been listening to CFRB on the taxi's radio. A plane has crashed into the World Trade Center!"

"Wow! That's quite something. How many killed? We should follow that one. Anyhow, back to work. Today we're going to look at writing for television. First, let's see if we can identify what makes bad TV writing."

That's as far as I got. The door opened again. It was the head of journalism training, Marilyn Mercer.

"It's unbelievable. Two planes have crashed into the World Trade Center. It's live on TV. They're blaming Al-Qaeda."

This was the biggest news story of the decade and, because of its global aftereffects some would argue, of the century. It was also one of the most scandalous moments in the history of CBC national radio. It waited a full hour before interrupting its scheduled program to tell its oblivious listeners about the events in New York and Washington. By then, almost every radio and TV station in the world, except CBC radio, had begun to cover the story. But it's not poor old CBC radio, a terrific service when it wants to be, that should come in for the most serious criticism. Since September 11, twenty-four-hour news has thrived on terror alerts, fear, half-truths, bombast and very short attention spans. The BBC still manages to maintain its professionalism in its main newscast, even-handed and generally unbiased, although it recently started slashing staff to save money. First to go: five hundred journalists. How very exhilarating. Now watch the domestic output descend to the level of its dreadful world TV service.

Or to the level of the U.S. networks or the pompous, self-important *New York Times*, which published Pentagon leaks as truth, insisting Saddam did have weapons of mass destruction and therefore it was right and proper for the U.S. to invade Iraq. Subsequent abject apologies have done little to restore the *Times'* credibility. Government spin had become its oxygen and the editors gasped it in with all the desperation of choking asthmatics. Relief was quick in those days. Another puff from the government inhaler, another front-page scoop from a reporter who believed every lie the Pentagon told her. More stunningly, she convinced her very superior superiors she was right and there was no need to get corroborating evidence, the most basic of all journalistic practices. But overuse of the inhaler put a strain on the paper's heart—its credibility. And slowly the truth sputtered out. On the nightly newscasts, the scripts began to omit the word "alleged" and all insurgents were branded "Muslim terrorists," although I don't recall any of them referring to Christian soldiers or Christian Humvees. However, there has been a journalistic upside: courageous reporting by British papers like the *Guardian* and the *Independent*; U.S. magazines such as *Harper's*, the *New Yorker* and *Atlantic* have done a superb job covering security, war and fear; so, too, has the PBS TV hour, *Frontline*. CBC TV News also did a great job on 9/11 with measured, powerfully understated reports.

But since Canada joined the so-called War on Terror, a lot of its reportage has resorted to jingoism, jolly-gosh reporting of Afghanistan, undercutting the mature coverage of 9/11. One story astounded viewers with the revelation that in the summertime, Afghanistan was really hot and the troops loved eating ice cream. And why is the reporting so amateurish? Because of a system invented by the U.S. called "embedding."

It has its official origins in the Persian Gulf War of 1991 when the media complained they were being kept too far from the action and were unable to report accurately. But it was in action long before that, though not so blatantly. In Vietnam, the U.S. media was generally credible and suspicious of the military propaganda. The daily, spin-filled late-afternoon news briefings in Saigon were universally known as the "Five O'Clock Follies." Yes, many newsmen and women did take rides on helicopters and go into battle with various platoons but, to the army's everlasting horror, there were few restrictions and little censorship. The truth was shown as well as the lies. And eventually, the truth emerged as the most powerful weapon that ended the insanity of this war.

But the U.S. military learned quickly from its harsh lessons of

Vietnam and realized it had to have the media, as well as the country, on its side. With a Republican White House, the spinning and the flag-waving became as natural as pies in a cow paddock. And the great communicator, Hollywood Ron, stood tall in his saddle as platitudinous home truths dribbled from his aw-shucks chops. Simple, old-fashioned home truths like good and evil and Commies and us. And it worked.

In the years after Vietnam, I remember working alongside the U.S. media in many parts of the world and was often astounded at how jingoistic, myopic and one-sided the reporting had become. It was no accident that the documentaries we made for the CBC's *The Journal* kept turning up on the American PBS Network and other stations around the world, hungry for a non-U.S. version of world events. In Beirut, one veteran CBS reporter salivated as he watched the documentary we were about to feed to Toronto. "God, I wish I could work for you guys. You really get to tell it how it is. I've got ninety seconds a night if I'm lucky, and then I have to put in what New York tells me. I'm in Beirut and they tell me what to report. And it's always this patriotic shit. They've made up their minds who the good guys are and that means the Palestinians are always wrong. It's such bullshit."

One veteran CBS reporter was so outraged in 2007, he wrote a blog in protest at what happened to him while covering Iraq. He and a crew had risked their lives to report on a terrible day, even by Baghdad's standards. Hundreds had been killed in one of the worst days of the war in a blizzard of car bombs, suicide attacks and rocket fire. The reporter and the CBS Baghdad bureau edited and voiced the tape and satellited it to their headquarters in New York.

"Oh, sorry, Baghdad, but we're going to have to drop you tonight. We've got a big story breaking here."

"What do you mean, you're dropping us? We risked our lives and got a fantastic piece that Americans need to see."

"I'm sorry, guys. But the story here's really big. Seven dogs have died eating tainted food."

That might not have happened at the CBC. It had earned itself a reputation for objectivity and technical excellence no matter how dangerous or difficult the conditions, and when abroad, little interference from Toronto. We certainly were not influenced by whatever side the U.S. happened to support.

Our independence and refusal to take sides was acknowledged in a subtle way in Beirut in June 1985, after Palestinian gunmen hijacked TWA Flight 847. You may remember the famous photograph of the pilot, John Testrake, leaning out the cockpit window with a gun held to his head. About forty passengers were taken hostage and then spirited away to secret hideouts around Beirut. After two weeks of negotiations, they were to be released and were gathered together in a compound before getting on buses to Syria. But the negotiators and organizers remembered the very first time they produced a hostage for the media at two in the morning at a hotel on the Cornice. I was there. The media behaved like madmen, shouting, jumping on tables and chairs, and terrifying the hostage. Never again, swore the officials. But they still wanted the world to see that the hostages had been well treated before they left for Syria. One crew and one crew only would be allowed in to get the pictures and interviews. That's all. The rest of you can get your material from them. Now who's it to be? A quick discussion among the dozens of crews and it was unanimous. "CBC." We got the world exclusive just by always trying to do our job, uninfluenced by patriotism or pride.

So after the Persian Gulf War of '91 and all the media complaints, the U.S. military switched tactics. Reporters and camera crews would get a chance to see war as never before. They would see it up close, just like the troops. They would be "embedded." That meant they lived, ate, slept and worked alongside the troops as they fought the enemy. But there were huge disadvantages. The military controlled what the media saw, when they saw it and how they reported it. These were new methods of propaganda and censorship. And, naturally, there was a bonding between the troops and the reporters that developed into a reliance on each other. The truth of war was lost in the fog of PR.

The argument now is that it is too unsafe for journalists to cover either Iraq or Afghanistan without the protection, guidance and rescue, if necessary, of the military. And that's exactly what the politicians and generals want. A media they can control and spin. Embedding in an evil that defies impartial reporting. It is an abnegation of objectivity and fairness, with only one side getting the coverage—the military. The "other" side, tens of thousands of bereaved, hungry, displaced and outraged Afghans and Iraqis have no place in Western coverage. It is bias of the most shameful kind. And we can blame the complicity of cowardly news executives, gouging insurance companies, the military and the politicians for hiding the ugly truths of war. How often do you hear that U.S. or Canadian forces have killed, say, forty insurgents? Can we see them? No. Why? It's too dangerous. Well, how do we know they are all Taliban, as you say? Are any of them civilians? Sorry, you'll just have to take our word for it.

Journalists are made to sign secrecy agreements before being embedded, and if they violate any part of the agreement, they are kicked out and sent home. That is probably the best thing that could happen, if only the media were smart enough to realize it. They could then, albeit dangerously (but that's part of our job), go about telling their real readers, listeners and viewers at home, the truth, and present opposing views to the sugar-coated, inflated patriotism to which they are constantly exposed while embedded.

Take this extract from a 2007 blog by an embedded reporter in Kandahar. Read it and ask yourself, with whom do his sympathies and affections lie? The soldiers, his audience, the people of Afghanistan or the Taliban? And, remember, while he is playing hockey with famous old names and his new military friends, he has ceased to be a professional journalist and just another victim of embedding.

> Seventeen former NHL stars were standing in the dirt, chatting to soldiers. The guys had been in Kandahar for almost 24 hours, arriving on a Canadian Forces C-130 Hercules transport plane. And they brought with them some pretty special cargo, the Stanley Cup.
>
> All this is meant to be a boost to troop morale. And the men and women wearing the (red, not blue) Maple Leaf on the shoulders of their desert camouflage could certainly use a bit of a break. Just over three weeks ago, eight of their own were killed in two separate explosions. And these soldiers are more than aware of the headlines

back home and the swirling controversy over how detainees handed over to Afghan authorities by Canadian troops are treated. Their tough-talking boss, Chief of the Defence Staff Gen. Rick Hillier, put it plainly: A lot of these men and women are "pissed off" that what they're doing on the ground is overshadowed by the detainee issue. Trooper Adam Poppy may not be as blunt as his boss, but as he lines up for his turn with the Stanley Cup, you can sense that this rotation in Kandahar hasn't been easy.

"We've had our ups and downs," he tells me, as he turns around and sees the hockey game behind him, and starts to smile. Mark Napier leans on his stick as he tells me why he helped organize this event. He wanted to see first hand how the mission was going. "Back home you hear so many negative things about the military and now you get over and find out it's not even close to what's portrayed," he says. The players spent more than an hour in the blistering heat, in a game that ended up very lopsided. Seven to one for the NHLers. But after the game is over, I walked up to the guy who let in those seven goals, Maj. Steve Bassindale. As he wipes his forehead, this senior officer says out of everything he's done during this rotation to Kandahar, standing in net, fielding shot after shot from guys who used to do this for a living, this is what will stand out for him when he remembers his time here.

When you hear an experienced military man say something like that, you know that for today at least, it's mission accomplished.

Notice how the reporter empathizes with the troops; after all, he's allowed to play hockey with his new buddies now. He opines they could certainly use a break; he describes the swaggering General Rick Hillier as "tough-talking" and accords him yet another platform for his draconian tactics of silencing all those who dare criticize the way Canadians treat their Afghan prisoners. On October 22, 2007, the CBC showed a revealing sixteen-second tape of Hillier arriving at Canada's Kandahar air base for a "surprise" four-day visit. The narration over the pictures by the anchor, Peter Mansbridge, said that Hillier was there to inspect new Leopard tanks, but he would not talk to reporters on his arrival. What the anchor should have said was that the reporters were prevented from asking any questions. The embedding system was the military's assurance of that. The tape shows Hillier, with an aide, walking across the tarmac and then, grinning widely, turning to his right to shout light-hearted banter to distant, unseen greeters—ladies and gentlemen of the embedded media rooted to their spots by orders of the military. As the tape ends, the camera widens a little to show Hillier shrugging, arms apart, hamming it up even more, gesturing, "It's not my fault, guys." And a smiling, sympathetic reporter waves back to his buddy, the general, indicating that's A-okay with him; he understands.

And a final point about that blog. Note the disturbing conclusion implying more than the hockey game: "Mission accomplished" is an unfortunate term clearly embedded in the blogger's mind as an acknowledgment of a military victory. He probably forgot about its most infamous use: as a somewhat premature banner behind George Bush on the aircraft carrier, USS *Abraham Lincoln*, in May 2003. But the reporter is a victim, too: A victim of a system that should be abolished, now.

Something else that should be abolished is the irresponsibility of conducting opinion polls in war zones and treating the results as facts. On October 18, 2007, Canada's *Globe and Mail*, the CBC and *La Presse* hit the nadir of ethical journalism when they published the headline: "Majority of Afghans want foreign troops to stay and fight." It appears that, because of the very high cost of polling, these three major organizations pooled their resources to try to con the public that they were, in fact, covering the war, whereas they were practicing one of the more loathsome pursuits in journalism—news by opinion poll. Opinion polls are dismissed by serious journalists because of their unreliability even in the most stable of democracies. They merely record a snapshot of a moment in time, and the picture that results is entirely dependent on the way the questions are phrased and to whom they are asked.

The poll in Afghanistan was done through translators, and the questions appeared too fashioned to elicit answers that would reflect well on the NATO mission. Yet, all three news organizations buried one astounding and revealing fact, if it, too, is to be believed: only 2 percent of those asked knew Canada had troops in the country. Indeed, those polled were members of a well-informed, credible populace who gave honest answers that presented the most current and reliable picture to date of the war in Afghanistan. And I'm a six-sided ham sandwich.

With all the cerebral sophistication of grade three tiddly-winks dropouts, the so-called senior management at the CBC, the *Globe* and *La Presse* convinced themselves that this was legitimate newsgathering. An opinion poll in Afghanistan. They even had the nerve to say the margin for error was 2.5 percent. And of course, people talking to a foreign pollster while under occupation are the likeliest on the planet to say exactly what they're expected to. They allegedly polled 1,600 people, although we will never know what the other thirty-one million thought. And yet this was trumpeted as responsible, legitimate journalism. And you and I are slapped in the face with this disregard for our own intelligence and our own need for proper reporting in Afghanistan.

→〉═ ● ═〈←

For a few minutes, let's go back to the carefree, jolly, happy, happy hours of journalists facing death before polls and embedding ruled the way we cover wars. It was a man's life in those good old days. Well, a woman's too. But I can't mention bedding or anything to do with sleeping materials or lateral positioning because a number of colleagues would even today want to remove certain still-but-only-barely valuable body parts of mine.

The weekend after 9/11 I was at home having dinner with my son, Jerome, and his partner, Antonio Alvarado, a Salvadoran who had seen the horrors of his country's twelve-year civil war, and, like tens of thousands of Latinos, had come north to find work so he could send money back to his impoverished family.

I wondered what Antonio thought of September 11.

"The world mourns because three thousand (mainly) Americans died. They killed eighty thousand of my countrymen and what do we hear? Nothing." Antonio, a beautiful, gentle man, uttered his judgment with bitterness and disgust, echoing the indigenous and the international revulsion at the manipulative, self-aggrandizing policies of the World's Policeman. Yet, five years later, many in the West still do not understand the *why* of September 11 and its successors, and fail to recognize the identities of the real global terrorists.

Let's go back to Antonio's country, El Salvador. It has a population of around seven million, but continuing inequities of land ownership and massive gaps between the few rich and the many poor plague the tiny country, just as they did when civil war erupted in 1980. In November of that year, Ron the Reagan was elected President of the United States. His inauguration was to be on January 23, 1981, and much was planned for that day for him and Nancy with the laughing face. Bands would march, fawns would speak and the chief justice would swear Ron in.

In El Salvador, a more robust celebration was planned: death, just for Ron. Death squads with names such as Sombra Negro, Black Shadow, had already killed their most dangerous opponents—four trouble-making nuns and an inquisitive crew from Dutch television. They also executed their most powerful and popular opponent, El Salvador's national martyr, Archbishop Oscar Romero who, in a national radio broadcast, had ordered the army to mutiny and to stop the killing "in the name of God." Romero railed against the U.S. for sending $1.5 million dollars *a day* in military aid for twelve years to support the ruling generals.

The day before his murder on March 24, 1980, by a government death squad gunman, he spoke for all the world's oppressed, after more massacres and desecration of churches, when he declared: "The persecution comes about because of the Church's defense of the poor, for assuming the destiny of the poor ..."

"Assuming the destiny of the of the poor"—for example, fighting on behalf of the Muslim Palestinians, or other poor and oppressed nations such as the Hindu Tamils of northern Sri Lanka, black South Africans or the *campesinos* of Central America.

A lunchtime volley of shots just yards from the Camino Real Hotel, in the capital San Salvador, brought death very close to us still alive in the foreign press corps. We saw the trademark Jeep Cherokee speeding away, leaving a university professor splattered on his pathway just behind the hotel. His wife screamed in horror. The professor's crime? Perhaps he thought too much or, worse, wrote too much. For him, though, the sword was much mightier than the pen.

The death squads were the tools of the right-wing henchman, Roberto D'Aubuisson, a.k.a., "Blowtorch Bobby" because of his favorite torture apparatus. He pledged to uphold law and order as perceived by the rich at the expense of the poor. But the peasants and cadres of the anti-government guerrilla group, the FMLN (*Farabundo Marti para la Liberacion Nacional*) were rumored to be planning something special of their own to coincide with Ron's inauguration.

As part of any familiarization tour of San Salvador, journalists would take a drive just out of town, up a winding hilly road that overlooked the city. Down in the gorge lay all the bodies dumped by the death squads after a hard night's work. No one tarried there and no one would identify the already yellowing corpses, fearing death by association. A few stray ones were left oozing on the sidewalks, but no more than two or three a night. At the city morgue, haunted mothers and wives stared at the fresh batch that had been brought in. Among the latest victims I saw something quite strange—a skinned baby duck. Wait a minute. That's not a baby duck; it's a male fetus sliced from its mother's stomach. A potential enemy of the state.

The man in San Salvador ran a great morgue. He couldn't do enough to help the foreign press. He had dozens more tucked away if we cared to take a look. Morgue-keepers are a gregarious, enthusiastic lot who take great pride in their work. At Moscow's main morgue just outside the city, the morgue man not only cheerfully introduced his overnight haul, he invited his guests to watch a cremation. In Kampala, Uganda, all their man could offer were a few slit throats and shoeless murder victims. Why do we go to morgues? To judge levels of ferocity and violence and to confirm or deny local claims about how many did or did not die that night.

From the morgue in San Salvador, it is about an hour's drive to the garrison town of Santa Ana, en route to the frontline fighting between the Salvadoran Army and the guerrillas. There had obviously been trouble in Santa Ana during the night. Bodies lay in the side streets and tense faces peered around every corner. We stopped at the gates of the local army barracks to ask for directions and perhaps get a pass to take to the government forward lines. Without warning, the guard pointed his M16 rife and screamed at us to get the fuck out of town or he would shoot. He was a mite tetchy because several of his buddies had been killed overnight and his commanding officer had defected to the guerrillas.

Our VW minibus was marked "TV," "Prensa," "CBC Canada," and we were flying a red and white maple leaf. We wheeled around and began to head back through the streets of Santa Ana en route to San Salvador. Bad move.

In El Salvador at the time, roughly 2 percent of the population owned 98 percent of the wealth. That was the root of the war. With pressure mainly from a guilty U.S. and Canada, President Napoleon Duarte had tried to start reforms, divesting the few of much of their land and handing it over to the poor. Santa Ana was home to several recently divested landowners. We did not know this.

The VW stopped outside the post office so reporter David Studer could call ahead to the President's office to confirm an interview scheduled for that afternoon. The rest of the crew followed David, mainly to stretch their legs. I stayed with the van and the gear. I became aware that a small crowd had silently gathered around the van. Suddenly a bleached face, wearing a monocle, reddened with fury as he charged up to me while I sat in the front passenger's seat.

He trembled with rage as he screamed in English: "You Canadians are traitors! Traitors! Where are the others? We saw them get out. Go and get them!"

"They're in the post office telephoning the President."

"Lies! Get them!"

Someone in the crowd had called the police, who arrived instantly in full battle dress with helmets, automatic rifles, pistols and grenades. One stepped up to the van and waved his M16 rifle, an order for me to open the back so he could search our TV gear. He then ordered the four Canadians and driver Luis Guidel back into the vehicle. Four paramilitaries took up positions at each corner of the VW, their guns trained on the passengers. In Spanish, one ordered Luis to reverse the van back to the police station about two hundred meters behind us. The crowd had grown, and they had begun chanting: "Kill them! Execute them!"

Not one of us said a word as the van crawled back toward the police station. It slowly sank in that we were in deadly trouble.

I thought about the martyred Romero, and the Maryknoll nuns who had been helping refugees flee the violence. According to the Maryknoll Sisters official statement, on December 2, 1980, members of El Salvador's National Guard intercepted the van carrying four American churchwomen as they were leaving the international airport in San Salvador. Maryknoll Sisters Ita Ford and Maura Clarke, Ursuline Sister Dorothy Kazel, and lay missionary Jean Donovan were taken to an isolated spot and shot dead. A UN report found the assassinations had been planned and were covered up by the Salvadoran military and U.S. officials.

But surely no one would kill an international television crew. But what about the four Dutchmen? They had traveled to the northern province of Chalatenango to link up with the rebels. Conflicting accounts say they were either killed in a government ambush or far more conveniently "killed in the crossfire" of a gun battle. One Dutch account says they were trailed by government gunmen who shot them with up to thirty bullets and then mutilated their bodies. There were no witnesses.

The only witnesses in Santa Ana were those who wanted to kill us. The van stopped but the chanting did not.

"Get out of the van! Up against the wall!"

"Kill them! Execute them!"

I glanced along the line, to see how the others were facing their final moments on this earth: veteran cameraman Bobby White was ashen and shaking; his much younger soundman, Rick Dubrocki, eyes glazed, looked dumbfounded; our driver, Luis Guidel, tried to light a cigarette but he was shaking too violently. The cigarette fell to the ground but he did not try to pick it up; David Studer stared straight ahead as if eye contact with any of us would confirm what he did not want to know—we were about to be executed.

Four rifles took aim at the foreign traitors.

How did I face my own execution?

The green trees behind the firing squad ruffled gently in the morning breeze. The sun was warm and I thought I was calm and at peace. Mouths were chanting but they made no sounds. So this is death. I didn't pray. I had no thoughts of home. A bullet in the head. That'll be okay. I can handle that. Okay. Okay. When are they going to shoot?

"What's going on here?"

A senior police officer had decided to take an early lunch. As he opened his office door he was confronted by the execution scene. He barked a few words to one of his men whose guns were still aimed at our heads. Then he, too, searched the van and found nothing incriminating—until he came across a research file that was crammed with telephone numbers, names of contacts, names of guerrillas and newspaper clippings about death squads.

That, I thought, had sealed our death warrants. There would be no reprieve.

Then he opened a copy of *Time* magazine and a smile crossed his face. He'd flipped to a page carrying an advertisement for "Beautiful Florida" that featured a blonde beach beauty wearing the tiniest bikini this guy had ever seen. He looked at the crowd, then to his men, then to us.

"Get the fuck out of here and never come back!"

She'll never know it, but that girl and her bikini had just saved five lives.

We left Santa Ana shaken but alive. A few kilometers outside the town, David did a piece to camera, recounting the drama. Then it was on with the rest of the day as though nothing had happened. We did get the interview with President Duarte that afternoon but, as I recall, it was full of platitudes and spin, not surprising as he was merely a puppet for the real commanders of El Salvador, the army, government death squads and U.S. advisors.

That night, we ate dinner at the Camino Real, had a few beers and a few glasses of wine, and celebrated our first day of taping in El Salvador. No one was yet ready to acknowledge what had happened in Santa Ana. I left the table early, as I felt a little unwell. As I got into the elevator I started to vomit violently. I don't think it was anything I ate.

→▬ ● ▬←

Just south of El Salvador lies Nicaragua.

Radio operators whispered code words to each other. "Puma, Puma, Puma."

"Leone, Leone, Leone."

"Puma, Puma, Puma."

"Leone, Leone, Leone."

In the dead of night in northern Nicaragua, very close to the Honduran border, a column of thirty men of the Sandinista army and a CBC *Journal* TV crew edged through the darkness. The army had an intelligence report that a band of Contras was laying an ambush in the mountainous jungle. The Sandinista's mission: kill the Contras before they killed them.

The Contras were troops that had been loyal to the deposed U.S.-backed dictator Anastasio Somoza and were fighting to win back their country with a great deal of secret help from Ron's White House (to be more respectful of the U.S. Commander in Chief—and that doesn't come easy—I should give him his proper title, Ronald Reagan, fortieth President of the United States of America). I seldom refer to that country as simply "America"—mostly "the U.S." or "United States" because to many other inhabitants of the continent of the Americas, for it to mean only the fifty states of the Stars and Stripes is insulting, dismissive and redolent of the swaggering superiority of a schoolyard bully.

Along with Ron was his cohort in crime, the crew-cut Colonel Oliver North, who lied to Congress about selling weapons to the alleged pariah state of Iran. Why did he sell weapons to Iran? Because the Iranians would be so grateful they would use their influence to win freedom for half a dozen hostages (mainly from the U.S.) chained to dungeon walls around Beirut. In turn, the money from those arms sales would then secretly go to the Contras, the Conservative "good guys" whom Ron and Ollie wanted to beat the "bad guys," the communist red socialist menace, the Sandinistas, just like in one of Ron's old movies.

The moon was high and full. Keeping a distance of twenty meters between each man, the patrol moved out very quietly. It would take all night to reach the ambush zone, but even now the soldiers were edgy. The ambush report may have been a ploy to lure them out into the jungle. The Contra attack could be sudden and soon.

We were only fifteen or twenty minutes out from base when I realized my pale jeans were glowing incandescently by the light of the silvery moon. I rubbed mud all over them but they still glowed like Las Vegas neon. And if they didn't see me, the Contras would surely hear me, because on my back was strapped a huge plastic container filled with clean drinking water that sloshed like the wake from a cruise liner hitting a dock. Every thirty minutes or so the column stopped. Then, in complete silence, crouched in a roadside ditch, not making a single move for about forty-five minutes. Cat and mouse, guerrilla style.

What was that? A rustling noise behind me. Then silence. There it was again! Contras? What do I do? Yell out a warning? No! Somebody will shoot me! Stay calm, stay calm. Stay in the ditch and don't move! Don't breathe! Closer this time. Couldn't be more than five meters behind me. One Contra? What if it's a whole unit? They've got guns. I haven't. What if they try to cut my throat? Oh, Jesus. If I don't yell out I'll be dead! Now just feet away. Just one. It sounded like just one.

I could hear his breath! Oh, *mierda!* He'll stab me! Christ! Silence again. Then he struck ... sniffed my twitching ear and, like all good dogs, ambled off in search of more playful company.

About three hours before dawn and close to ambush alley, the patrol leader called halt.

"Get some rest. We'll hit them as the sun comes up."

There was a bit of a hitch, though. The sleeping site was atop a very steep, wet hill. It was like trying to climb up a kid's slide that had been coated with oil. Two steps up, then—Whoa!—back to the bottom—camera, gear, water container and all. Four steps up, then … whoa again! Back to the bottom. The heavily armed soldiers nimbly picked their way to the top and were fast asleep as four mud-caked Canadians continued rocketing down the hillside, sleepless in the sierras.

Sun-up was not the usual cool mountain dawn—already the day was a burning furnace as the hunt for the Contras resumed through mile after mile of hills, thick brush and barren rocks. El Señor Jefe Scully and his merry hombres, David Donnelly, David Pickoski and Ann Medina, were struggling. The heat, exhaustion, lack of sleep, lack of food, plus fear and tension were taking their toll, every step becoming more difficult than the last. And the Sandinistas bounded on.

"Puma, Puma, Puma."

"Leone, Leone, Leone."

The forward scouts had no fresh intelligence. Had they made a mistake and bypassed the Contras who were waiting in ambush for the main patrol? Were we already in their gun sights?

"Puma, Puma, Puma."

A muffled reply: "Leone, Leone, Leone. No enemy in the area. Return to base."

Shit!

→━● ● ━←

The military leader of the Contras was a Sandinista hero turned rebel, Eden Pastora. His nom de guerre was Commandante Zero who operated out of a base camp in southeastern Nicaragua.

Getting to meet him was difficult. First, as the producer with the CBC *Journal* crew, I had to rent a small plane in San José, Costa Rica, to fly us with a dozen cases of camera gear to the mouth of the Rio Coco that forms a natural border with Nicaragua. Then came a two-day boat trip. The boat was a thirty-foot flat-bottomed floating junk heap with an outboard motor that kept breaking down, a small canvas canopy, and a surly boatman.

On the first night, the boatman edged his craft to a riverbank and announced this was where dinner would be eaten and the night would be spent. We clambered up a muddy bank to find a small, wooden shack. The restaurant on the river bend must have been built for passing television crews because there was no sign of other life for miles and miles. Our crew sat at the only table as a kerosene lamp flickered into life to reveal a scrawny old chicken being served by a scrawny old lady. At least the chicken seemed to be cooked ... I'm not so sure about her.

The next day, after another eight hours, our floating palace glided into Commandante Zero's base camp. But he wasn't there. Gone. Word had been sent ahead that the CBC was coming but he had more important things to do, like fight a war. The few soldiers still at the camp did not object to being filmed as they trained, shot fish and handled boats. It was hardly award-winning tape, but it would make a mildly interesting forty seconds in the documentary that would include a piece to camera, here, by reporter Bruce Garvey.

Back on the boat, which was breaking down on the half hour, the boatman started asking for more money because the voyage was taking longer than he had estimated. He failed to understand or concede that it was his fault because his engine kept breaking down. The argument went on long into the night, echoing down the mighty Rio Coco.

"Give me more money!"

"Fuck off!"

"I want more money!"

"Fuck off."

He lost, the CBC won. Oh, yeah?

A week later there was an attack on Zero's camp. He had invited another group of journalists based in Costa Rica to pay him a visit. As the press gathered around, someone hurled a grenade in an attempt to assassinate him. Zero was not badly injured but two journalists were killed. Two weeks later, the local newspaper, *La Republica*, published a two-page story on its findings after a major investigation into the incident, and they named a prime suspect who had fled the scene: me.

The story said that Mr. John Scully of the Canadian Broadcasting Corporation had hired a plane, giving its correct registration number and the exact cost of the charter, at San Jose and had gone to Zero's camp. Mr. Scully, who lived at XX Alberta Avenue, in Toronto, Canada (correct), and whose telephone number was 416-XXX-XXXX (correct), was seen loading silver cases onto the plane, implying at the very least that I had a role in the assassination. The camera cases could have been crammed with grenades, and the description of their suspect was also correct: fair complexion, fair hair. Martha Honey, a correspondent with the *New York Times,* phoned me the morning the story was printed and asked if any of this were true. Was the CBC involved in the grenade plot? Were you involved? No. We were back in Toronto when the assassination attempt was made.

So, where had all this information come from? Why? And how come everything was meticulously correct except that, conveniently, no one had checked the date of the charter flight against the date of the assassination attempt? I remembered that while we were in San José, a source identified another guest at the Hotel Irazu as the CIA station chief, but I thought no more about it until *La Republica*'s story. Then the penny dropped from a great height. As the senior field producer for the CBC's *The Journal*, I had produced several documentaries in Central America that could have been interpreted as critical of the U.S. and its policies in the region. These documentaries were also seen on PBS, the U.S. Public Broadcasting Service, possibly Washington's most-watched channel. Someone in a high place had wanted to shut the CBC up.

Now it appears that whoever tossed the grenade was linked to the Sandinista Intelligence Service and wanted Zero out of the way. Although he'll never know it, the boatman would get his revenge, too.

Six months later, vindicated and absolved, I had erased this chapter from my memory banks when I felt a twinge on my right side near my lower ribs. Within three hours I had collapsed and was rushed to the Sunnybrook Medical Centre in Toronto. The emergency staff was mystified. They had no idea what was causing my temperature to soar way over the hundred mark; nor could they explain the intensity of the pain that allowed me to breathe only in short gasps. Then a lung collapsed and I was moved into the Special Care Unit where a nurse inserted a morphine drip. A junior doctor who had an interest in tropical medicine suggested to his superiors that it might be something the patient picked up in Central America.

"Don't be stupid. We think he's got a blood clot, so we're putting him on thinners. And we'll up the morphine."

But I got worse, and senior doctors, unable to control the pain, pondered cutting nerves that were feeding into their rapidly declining patient's brain. Then they had "the talk" with my wife, Toni. She went home and broke the news to our kids, Jerome and Emma.

But that junior doctor and my very aggressive family doctor refused to "let nature now take its course." They wheeled me down to ultrasound for the fifth time, ensnared in a tangle of tubes, oxygen masks and drips. A massive asthma attack added a certain charm to the afternoon theater.

"What's that?" demanded Pam Letts, my GP. "That lump there! What is it?"

"Ah, we haven't seen that before."

"Well, do a biopsy!" ordered pushy Dr. Letts.

Their resentment was tangible, even through a fog of morphine and Ventolin; but they agreed. In went the needle and out came a mass of poison. A liver abscess! Yes, oh joy, we've found a liver abscess. Hooray for us!

They were right, of course. It was an amoebic liver abscess caused by a parasite living a life of great luxury in my, er, stools. And how does one normally contract such an abscess? Commonly by eating poorly cooked chicken. I wasn't the only victim. Our translator, Marcello Montecino, also nearly died of exactly the same thing. Medically, it's called an amoebic liver abscess, but I know one translator and one producer to whom it will always be known as the Boatman's Revenge.

The killings in Central America go on to this day, thanks only in part to the drug gangs. In Fort Benning, Georgia, there's a school that trains Central American military. It was established fifty years ago, and until 2001 was known as the U.S. Army School of the Americas; its more infamous Spanish acronym was the SOA. So bad had its reputation become for turning out torturers, death squads and human rights violators in countries such as El Salvador, Guatemala and Colombia, Congress pressured the SOA to clean up its act or it would be closed. The U.S., which pays ten million dollars a year to train its terrorist surrogates, was not going to allow that to happen. Instead, the Pentagon changed the name of the school to the Western Hemisphere Institute for Security Cooperation, and published a manifesto that ostensibly heralded a new era in the Institute's attitude to human rights. But nothing has changed and it still churns out killers who keep right-wing, U.S.-friendly dictatorships in power though murder, torture and corruption. It is no surprise to anyone in Guatemala that in the run-up to the 2007 elections, death squads executed forty adversaries in just a few weeks. And it was no surprise they included nineteen candidates, plus children, spouses, journalists and union leaders.

At the same time, up to thirty candidates were murdered during Colombia's regional election campaign. The government automatically blamed the FARC terrorists, but there is reason to suspect that whomever President Uribe didn't like would also be killed. As a result, a number of candidates withdrew from the election, choosing to remain among the dead silent as opposed to silent dead.

Evo Morales, the indigenous president of Bolivia, says he will stop sending any of his military to Fort Benning because it teaches officers how to confront their own people and identify social movements as evil. Morales was no doubt influenced by an event in his country in 2006. Two former SOA graduates were arrested on charges of torture, murder and violation of the constitution for their responsibility in the death of sixty-seven civilians during the so-called "Gas Wars" of 2003. The fight was over plans to export natural gas to the United States through a port in Chile. For the locals, it was just another example of foreign exploitation of Bolivia's natural resources, particularly by Sam the Plundering Man.

And you thought the United States really and truly wanted to spread democracy around the world? Now you know just a little bit better. It's like that abscess, festering away until it erupts, causing pain and death.

4

Saddam the Terrible

Baghdad has become an abscess and it, too, has had other names. It is either Aramaic for "sheep enclosure" or, rather more tastefully, ancient Persian for "the gift of God." If the Persian is right, then it's about time He took it back.

Baghdad was part of the Turkish Ottoman Empire until it was mandated to the British at the end of the First World War. Iraq became independent in 1932 but the Brits invaded it again in 1941. They left after the Second World War and it became a monarchy until the army overthrew the king, with continuing support from the Soviets. The major powers all wanted in on Iraq's action because of two things: its strategically important location, bordering Turkey, Iran, Syria, Saudi Arabia and the Persian Gulf; and oil. Wouldn't you do all in your power, however nasty, to drive them out and keep them out?

In 1979, enter Saddam Hussein Abd al-Majid al-Tikriti, born 1937. Before capture: height 1.86 m, trousers 54, jacket 56, outside leg 112 cm, shirt XL, shoe 45, number of opponents executed by his secret police during his twenty-four-year regime: up to half a million. Mr. Hussein has never been a good boy, unless it was the time he was getting the Americans to supply him with chemical and other weapons to kill the Iranians. Then he was a genuine sweetie pie. Reagan even gave him forty billion to fight the bad fight. The Soviets loved him at first, too, and gave him arms and advisors. And what about the French? They gave him the technology to enrich uranium and build a nuclear reactor. The Israelis put a stop to that with an air strike.

And so what if he killed a few thousand Shia Muslims who rose against him after the first Gulf War, drained their marshlands, gassed Kurds, meaninglessly sacrificed hundreds of thousands of his own soldiers in a war against Iran? And sure, he had innocent folks tortured and jailed, especially if they didn't belong to his Sunni Muslim minority religion, even when Saddam himself was not a holy man, but a secular sybarite to whom religion was simply a way of deciding who to kill. But hey, isn't that what a good dictator does? And they put him on trial for just doing his job, just like they did to poor old Mr. Milosevic, who had the sense to die before being found guilty. (Kenneth Lay and General Augusto Pinochet were copycats.) I wonder what would happen to other alleged perpetrators of mass death, like U.S. former secretary of state Henry Kissinger (South America, Southeast Asia, East Timor) or Meles Zenawi of Ethiopia, Than Shwe of Burma, or Augusto Pinochet of Chile and Pol Pot (they took the Lay way, too) if they ever got to The Hague.

But Hussein was a good man, or so his suave, gray-haired lackey of a foreign minister, Tariq Aziz, insisted to us as we set up for an interview before Saddam's brilliant tactical move to invade Kuwait, a move that ended up wiping out most of Iraq's army.

From the moment we arrived in Iraq, we were assigned two "minders" who made sure we saw nothing the government did not want us to see, such as military maneuvers, billboards that did not feature Saddam, streets that had cars in them (huh?) and bridges, especially no bridges. They shared paranoia about filming bridges with India. Film a bridge and they shoot you because bridges are tactical installations and the enemy might see the tape and guess the location of the bridge. It didn't seem to occur to either of these geniuses that millions of pedestrians and cars cross these bridges every year; they're in guidebooks, road maps and are some of the best-known structures in the country.

And not just bridges. During the eight-year Iran-Iraq war, that cost a million lives and ended in stalemate, the CBC was given permission to travel to the port city of Basra, which the Iranians had just attacked. That was February 1984.

The road from Baghdad to Basra was an unrelieved brown, hypnotic mudscape. After five hours of it we arrived around 2:00 PM. We told our minders we would like to start shooting right away.

"Now? You want to start now?"

"Yeah, it's already two o'clock, and it's five hours back to Baghdad, so let's get going."

One of the unusually perplexed minders suggested we first meet the general. Okay.

"You have driven all that way and we have such a nice lunch prepared. First we eat. Then we go."

"But General, we are worried about the light. If we wait here too long it will be dark."

"No, no, my friend. Come. We eat." The meal consisted of ducks, sheep, cows, fish, pasta, cheese, hummus, pita bread, cake, vegetables, tea, coffee, juice and then around we went again. This was all part of the Iraqi plan: invite them to Basra to keep them out of the way and then block them.

The meal took two hours and explained why so many of the Iraqi officers were far from lean and hungry, unlike today's warriors, domestic or imported. At four o'clock the general rose and announced: "We go right now. You see, my friend, there is plenty of light."

"Thank you, General. Now, if you could just wait a moment or two, we'll get the camera gear from the car."

"Camera? No, no. No cameras are allowed."

Oh, dear. Al-ibn-bin-Scully-al-Toronto was about to unload, and not his lunch.

"General! We have permission from the foreign ministry in Baghdad. Here's the letter. We would not have come if cameras were not allowed. We work for t-e-l-e-v-i-s-i-o-n!"

"No. You obey me, not Baghdad."

As a journalist, I could not let him win so easily. He was censoring us even before we had begun filming. I had to go for broke … as in arms or legs. And I did the culturally unforgivable. I shook my finger at him.

"Listen, General, we had a deal with your government to see the damage and film it. That was the deal. So can we please go now? With our camera!"

The lippy Canadian could either be shot or sentenced to a life contemplating the mudscape. But it worked! Sort of. The general deployed a total of seventeen plainclothes bullyboys whose sole job was to block the camera. We were not allowed to film damage, factories or people. Yes, you can film the cargo ships tied up at the docks, but nothing else. Not that naval destroyer; not that minesweeper. As the camera rolled on the now sanitized dock, the seventeen bullyboys formed a V behind the tripod. As

Mike Sweeney slowly panned over in the direction of the naval boats, into the shot came ten minders; pan left, the other seven. No fools, these boys. They had clearly outsmarted many crews before us, and they had just censored another one.

But for all that, the Iraqi officers with whom we mingled were a sentimental lot. Big, over-lunched bellies with real soft hearts. Sure, they sent half a million kids to the front to be fodder for the Iranians, but this was war. And the next day also happened to be the birthday of our soundman, Alister Bell. Now what would he like for a gift, one of them asked? Hmm.

The next morning, there was a gleam in the general's eye as we skimmed over the deserts and mountains in a Russian-made helicopter. Yes. He had the perfect gift for Al.

The chopper landed and a jeep drove us up a series of gravel roads until it reached the Iraqi army's forward artillery position. All morning, in bitter winter winds, the big guns had pounded the Iranians ten kilometers away across a mountain gully, but had stopped for a spot of lunch. Surprise, surprise, no you can't film the guns but—and here it came—we have a surprise for the birthday boy! How would he like to operate an artillery gun? Fire a few shells at the Iranians!

We could see the headline: "CBC Soundman Kills 20 Iranian Soldiers and Destroys Two Villages as He Pummels Opposing Army. Way to Go, Al." Uh, thanks, but no thanks.

"But he must. It's our gift to him. He cannot refuse."

"Tell you what, let us film the guns as Al's birthday present. You will make him very happy and proud that you have honored him in this manner."

"Okay. Okay. What would you like us to hit?"

"Nothing! We would just like to get a few shots of the guns and the men preparing for action. That would be fine."

"You don't want us to shoot? It's no problem. We can kill some Iranians for you."

"No, no. Not just for us. But are you going to fire anyway? Because then we could film."

"No. We are waiting for some new coordinates but we can use the ones we had this morning."

"Uh, no, it's okay. But thanks for the offer. So we can go ahead and film the guns and the men without them firing?"

"Okay. Okay." The reply was glum and mystified.

That night in the city of Kirkuk, the Iraqi army got even. "CBC! CBC! Over here! You come to this table. We've got cake for Mr. Al."

They had more. On the table were several bottles of local firewater, a Pernod–Araq–Iraq kind of brew that could have saved them thousands of dinars in jet fuel. The toasting went on long into the night.

Al had his birthday.

The CBC Four were a sick bunch of pixies the next day.

Al should have fired the gun.

Back in Baghdad, one of our official minders—I'll call him Abbas—came to my hotel room a couple of days before our flight to London. First, he turned on all the taps, the shower, the radio and the TV. He said every room in the Al-Rashid hotel was bugged.

"Mr. John, I must talk to you," he whispered. "You are my only hope. I am going to ask you for something and you must say yes."

"What is it, Abbas?"

He slipped a photograph from his inside pocket.

"This is my girlfriend. I met her in London two years ago and I want to marry her. I love her very much and she loves me, but we cannot be together."

Abbas was about thirty, small, slim and gentle, with a soft voice, and tormented by the thought of not seeing his girlfriend again.

"But Abbas, why don't you just buy a ticket and fly to London? Don't you have the money?"

"No, no. It's not the money. Because I am in the secret police, I am not allowed to leave Iraq now. They think I know too much. I don't, but they think so. They will put me in jail if they suspect I am trying to leave."

"So what do you want from me?"

"Mr. John, you must get me a Canadian passport, that's the first thing. Then an air ticket. I know the airport very well and I know how to get around all the formalities. I know every door and every exit. I can avoid everyone. I just say I'm part of the CBC crew and I join you at the bottom of the steps of the plane and merge with you and there will be no more problems."

Was this a setup? A trap to get us thrown out of the country? Or thrown in jail for filming things we weren't supposed to? I wasn't sure. A week earlier, we had accidentally come across a huge military convoy heading toward Basra: tanks, heavy guns and rockets. We filmed it. Later, an official at the Canadian Embassy wanted to know all about that convoy. Could we keep our eyes open for anything else and report it to him? Dream on, sunshine. But why did the embassy want to know? Could it be they were in the spy business? Oh, no. Don't be silly.

I looked at the pathetic Abbas and asked myself again if he was setting us up, getting us caught aiding and abetting a defector? I think I believed him. But it was not a chance I could take. There is no way we could be connected with any illegal activity, especially at the security-obsessed airport. The Iraqis wouldn't take kindly to that. Oh, no. And Toronto would not have been thrilled either. I didn't think I had a choice.

"Abbas, I'm sorry, but the CBC cannot get involved in that sort of thing."

"But," he pleaded, "surely you can get me a Canadian passport!"

"No. I'm sorry."

I don't know what happened to Abbas. I hope he wasn't censored, too.

5

Dirty Gael Talk

In Belfast, the censors were often men who could put two pennies in a phone box: "Are yoos from the BBC?"

"Yes. My name is John Scully; I'm the national TV news producer here in Belfast. Who's speaking, please?"

"Never mind that. Yoos all fookin' bastards. And yoos will be very sorry." Click.

Welcome to Belfast, and as the Anglo-Irish comedian Spike Milligan would reply:

"And you're welcome to it, too, mate."

Northern Ireland's population is around two million. Just over half are Protestant, just under half, Roman Catholic. Ireland has been inhabited for about nine thousand years. A little more recently it was colonized in the 1600s by Scottish and English Protestants who seized political and social rights from the local Catholics.

They forced the Catholics off their land, onto the street or onto tiny plots where they planted their only food, the potato, a vegetable that had become the staple food for peasants throughout Ireland. Then came Ireland's own September 11, that lives on in bitterness and hatred to this day. September 1846. Blight hit the potato crop. The Great Potato Famine lasted four years. British landlords evicted the living from their shacks because they couldn't pay the rent. In 1847 alone, one hundred thousand dragged themselves onto the so-called "coffin ships" to escape to Canada and the U.S. One in five destitute, sick and hopeless emigrant Irish men, women and children died of disease and malnutrition. At the same time, English landlords chartered cargo ships that sailed away from Irish shores laden down with mutton, oats, wheat, poultry and beef for Europe and the U.S., where they could get better profits.

The Irish ate grass and weeds until a million of them were dead.

Up until then, the Catholics had formed a number of insurgent movements, out of which grew the Irish Republican Brotherhood that launched the abortive Easter Rebellion of 1916 and its Proclamation of Independence, which in part states:

> We declare the right of the people of Ireland to the ownership of Ireland, and to the unfettered control of Irish destinies, to be sovereign and indefeasible. The long usurpation of that right by a foreign people and government has not extinguished the right, nor can it ever be extinguished except by the destruction of the Irish people. In every generation the Irish people have asserted their right to national freedom and sovereignty: six times during the past three hundred years they have asserted it in arms. Standing on that fundamental right and again asserting it in arms in the face of the world, we hereby proclaim the Irish

Republic as a Sovereign Independent State, and
we pledge our lives and the lives of our com-
rades-in-arms to the cause of its freedom, of its
welfare, and its exaltation among the nations.

Note the phrase "the long usurpation ... by a foreign people
and government," the classic raison d'être for many insurgencies.
The failed Easter Rebellion was followed by violent guerrilla war
fought by the newly named Irish Republican Army, the IRA, to
end British rule. In 1920, the south became the Independent
Republic of Ireland. The north was granted home rule, answer-
able to the British Monarch and the British Parliament. Irish
nationalists and their military brothers in the IRA did not accept
this division and bloodily fought for unification throughout
much of the twentieth century. Renewed "troubles" in 1969
brought twenty thousand British troops to Northern Ireland to
try to maintain law and order. Even so, over three thousand died
in bombings, riots, shootings and executions. Political prisoners
starved themselves to death after being held in detention without
trial. Both the IRA and its main Protestant counterparts, the Ulster
Defence Association (UDA) and Ulster Volunteer Force (UVF)
fomented a vicious war of bigotry backed by guns. By the early
twenty-first century, a series of Westminster-brokered peace accords
eased the violence, and most of the warring parties surrendered
their weapons.

It is now impolite to remember that the Irish Republican
Brotherhood and the IRA fought for food, land and justice, and
not religion. The world had condemned them as terrorists. But
because of their armed struggle, the Republic of Ireland has

become an economic giant in Europe. So were the IRB and IRA really terrorists or were they, in fact, true freedom fighters?

The BBC building in Belfast is a six-storey neo-Georgian landmark on the Ormeau Road. It was opened in 1941 and, to the delight of local Protestants, its first television broadcast was the coronation of Queen Elizabeth II in 1953. During the troubles, it was a target to both sides, and the bombers made several unsuccessful attempts to do more than just shake its very sturdy foundations. It had been specially reinforced and its windows were covered with heavy bars and wire netting. As a result, damage during the troubles was slight by Belfast standards—some broken glass and a few splintered spirits.

Just opposite the BBC stood a bland, brick office building where workers came in unremarkably at nine and left again on their anonymous journeys at five. Monday to Friday. Around lunchtime one Monday, I glanced out of the window and was met with the oddest sight. They were all running out of the building with big, wide grins on their faces. I guessed it was just another evacuation drill … until the bomb exploded. Those grins are better known to terrorists and doctors as *rictus*, faces frozen in hysterical terror. The bomb shook the entire block and blasted the building to pieces. I dived under my desk in case our building went up, too, but the BBC would not surrender. I don't know how many of those faces ended up on cemetery markers. I do know that it was only the first bomb of the day. Five more turned Belfast city center into crushing walls of flame and orange death. In that gross, simplistic statement used by journalists the world over, the IRA "claimed responsibility" for the bombs. It was probably true, but what was the verification? A code word used by an anonymous voice in a phone call to the police. More recently, claims of violence come via the Internet. The more horrific, the more chilling the deed or threat, the more likely it is to be "confirmed" by Washington or London as "authentic" and, like grateful supplicants, most journalists buy the story and use it without question. It is probably terribly unpatriotic to ask questions about counter-terrorism tactics or to suggest that all may not be what it appears.

But I digress. So the IRA took the blame for the Belfast bombings. In an earlier incident outside Londonderry, the Protestant UVF claimed responsibility for the execution of two lovers. They were in the young boy's car, parked in a deserted country lane. Yes, both sides in the Irish struggle were God-fearing and sin-free, fighting in the name of the Lord, but it wasn't that the UVF took umbrage at the two having pre-marital sex in the back seat of a car. They were enraged that one lover was Protestant, the other Catholic. Gunshots to the head put a stop to that but there was more of God's work to be done: the boy's penis was hacked off and stuffed in his mouth; the girl's stomach was sliced open and his testicles inserted.

In Londonderry itself, nothing polarized the madness more than Bloody Sunday. It's a dim memory now, that awful day petrified among the musicology and mythology of tragic, vainglorious Ireland. Yeats's "terrible beauty" was born again on Sunday, January 30, 1972.

A peaceful civil rights march by Catholics through the suburban Bogside was watched over by the British Army's elite 1st Battalion, the Parachute Regiment, the tough-boy Paras—cold, hardened professionals who heard a crack of gunfire, or so they told a Royal Commission of Inquiry, and they returned fire, killing thirteen unarmed civilians. Bloody Sunday was a human hell but it had its journalistic triumphs.

The television pictures were a testament to courage. BBC cameraman Cyril Cave was caught between the Paras and their victims. Flat, face-down on the road, he kept his camera rolling as the gunshots cracked over him. Then he belly-crawled to rejoin his soundman, Jim Deany, and reporter John Bierman. He slapped the film magazine into John's hands and John took off on a seventy-mile maniacal drive back to Belfast where the film had to be processed. He arrived at 5:35 PM. The news was on at six. It took twenty minutes for the chemicals to turn meaningless shiny celluloid into frames of madness that flicked by at the rate of twenty-four per second. Five minutes to air. A sprint from the film lab across the street, up five flights of stairs into telecine, the projection room. No time for even a rudimentary edit, no time to write a script, no time to be checked by the producers in London, who knew that this was a volatile and dangerous story that would enrage and inflame more hatred and more death. There was no time to verify accusations that the army had, in fact, massacred those thirteen unarmed marchers in cold blood. But the clock owned the rights to everyone's soul. They went live. With just his memory, a few scribbled notes and Cyril Cave's brave film, Bierman, gaunt and outraged, ad-libbed the script, factual yet damning, jagged slices of words and sound that chiseled another epitaph as the pornography of Ireland flickered by on the six o'clock news.

The British named Brigadier Lord Chief Justice Widgery to head an inquiry into Bloody Sunday. He was appointed by Prime

Minister Edward Heath, who allegedly held a secret meeting with the incorruptible fellow member of the Establishment to remind him that a military and propaganda war was being fought in Northern Ireland. He exhorted Widgery "to do the right thing." Widgery got the message, accepted perjury as truth and rushed out a report that exonerated the British Army from any blame. The howls of "whitewash" were so intense that the British government was forced to launch another inquiry. The disgraced Widgery died of dementia in 1981.

The hardest part of being a journalist in any war zone is knowing who or what to believe. Northern Ireland was no different. British Army PR flaks would drape themselves over the bar and feed disinformation to the press staying in the world's most bombed hotel, the Europa (twenty-eight times by a recent count, and it has been renamed the Forum). The bunny girls in the Penthouse dining room didn't miss a beat as they tended their litter, who could watch Belfast burn as they lapped up their Irish coffees and nibbled away at army tidbits and bunny tails.

The Penthouse was for the "foreign" press, army brass and wealthy bon vivants. It was not for the likes of big, burly Billy. I cannot tell you his last name because Billy was our paid informer, our early warning system. He was about thirty and a member of the Protestant Ulster Defence Association. We, the BBC, paid him twenty-five pounds a week as our undercover consultant-in-residence. Well, snitch. He would tell us if the latest assassination was for nationalistic or religious reasons, or if the victim hadn't paid that week's protection money, or if he had reneged on a drug deal. Business was booming along with the bombs. There was the gun trade, the bomb trade, the kidnapping trade, the drug trade, the hate trade. Civil war is heaven-sent if you know how to exploit it.

Billy was on the payroll for about six months. He disdained secrecy and security and would turn up at the BBC in the bright light of an Irish afternoon to pick up his pay. Then someone blabbed ... Billy, probably. My guess is he just had to tell his mates that he was a very important man and "have a drink on me." That was when one of the London tabloids front-paged the story: "Protestant Informer Paid By BBC." The story included Billy's full name, my full name and the names of several other producers and reporters.

We took the next phone threat very seriously and all of us BBC National News folk left hurriedly for London. Billy? Billy was found dead a few days later. And, no, it wasn't an accident.

Hand and Foot Note:

On the outskirts of Belfast in the unlikely named suburb of Hollywood simmered one the city's best restaurants. A half-hour taxi ride through the darkened streets, past army patrols and other guns peering at passers-by through unseen windows. I had a reservation. Rang the bell and pulled on the door. And pulled. And *pulled*. Until the handle was in my grip. Ripped from it moorings. And a stricken owner standing aghast. "It opens inwards, sir. Inwards."

Humiliation was never a deterrent so the next night I went back. The food had been good, the wine probably more so because I don't remember it. But now I knew the secret code. Ring the bell and push the door. It worked brilliantly. As I basked in my dextrous glory and sauntered confidently to the maitre d's softly lit desk, I kicked over the entire set of fireplace accouterments:

brass shovel, brass poker, brass stand. The clanging and jangling reverberated across the restaurant and beyond the shores of the Irish Sea.

"Ah," said the owner, "Mr. Scully. Good evening. I hear you've arrived."

6

South of the Border

We retuned to Ireland many times during the troubles, which tormented the north with infinitely more brutality than the independent Republic of Ireland in the south. The IRA ran its campaigns from both countries but its political wing, Sinn Fein, always held its annual convention in Dublin, not Belfast.

In the north, the center of Belfast was a fortress of barricaded streets and malls caged in by security turnstiles and patrolled by heavily armed members of the mainly Protestant Royal Ulster Constabulary and ubiquitous "pigs" of the British army. Now, now, I'm not abusing the Brits, not this time, anyhow. In army talk, a "pig" was a big, old, obsolete armored personnel carrier. It was built onto a Humber truck chassis and shook the bejeezus out of the eight to ten soldiers inside. It was called a pig because its front looked like a porker's snout and it drove, well, like a pig. But once inside the security cordon, and if you knew the right shop, you could find a feast of IRA propaganda, from the bitter freedom songs of the old Fenian brigades to newer, scratchy LPs on which men inside the Maze internment camp produced rousing anti-British ditties like "The Men Behind The Wire." Tricolors and copies of the Proclamation of Independence were de rigueur.

It did occur to me that everyone who entered the store would have been photographed and filed on a secret data bank, but what the hell, the shop itself was probably a front run by the Brits.

In the south, the difference was startling. No military on the streets, no chained-in shopping centers. But the Irish secret police were active. I know because I inadvertently got drunk with one of them. A difficult chore, I have to admit. We had come the Republic to shoot a documentary on how the fighting in the north was affecting life and politics in the south. And I'd heard that the Irish navy was patrolling offshore, searching for ships running weapons from Europe and dropping them off at secluded coves in both the north and the south. In fact, I knew one of the gunrunners personally. He was not European but was the main supplier of everything from ArmaLite rifles for the IRA, AK-47s for the Protestant militias, and further afield, much bigger and more cataclysmic weapons for India and Pakistan. He is still alive, as is his family. I suspect if I named him, that status would abruptly change.

The Irish spook's cover was that of a medium-ranking functionary in the military who would arrange for us to go on patrol with the Irish navy. The catch was he wanted to meet for lunch on a Saturday. Unusual for a bureaucrat to work on the weekend, especially just to have lunch with a Canadian journalist, even if his name did have Irish lineage.

First it was a couple of shots of Bushmills Irish Whiskey. Just to set the mood. Lunch at this exclusive Dublin restaurant began with a third Bushmills, then a sumptuous feast accompanied by several bottles of expensive, very good wine. My man kept talking to me about the great work the Irish police and navy were doing and what did I think of the events over the border? Did I know anyone involved? Surely as a journalist you must meet all sorts. Now what's this documentary about? Oh, wait. It's time for a wee Irish coffee. You like Irish coffee, John? That's grand. No, no, no. It's all on me. It's a privilege to have a wonderful lunch with such a well-respected journalist like yourself. Why don't we have just one more?

We left the restaurant at 4:30, but whether it was AM or PM I have no recollection.

Nor have I any idea if I drunkenly blabbed anything of worth to my ebullient and generous spook. But at least he had checked me out and probably discovered that I was just another freeloading hack who bored him to tears. At least, I hope that's the impression I left.

Three days later, as my hangover lifted, we went to sea with the Irish navy. The patrol did stop a few fishing boats but found no caches of weapons hidden beneath the decks of the Spanish, Portuguese and Irish fishing boats bobbing around the Irish Sea.

Then we headed inland to interview some folks in County Cork. It was a (and I'm not making this up) misty, wet Irish night. We had driven from Dublin, bound for a reputedly gorgeous old hotel near Cork, but we were running very late. I reckoned we wouldn't reach it until eleven. I'd better phone ahead. It appeared that someone had a vendetta against the telephone company because all the phone boxes had been stolen. Well, we couldn't find one. Ah, but there's a friendly old Irish pub, looking more like a quaint cottage filled with good cheer. A "Harp Lager" sign glowed over the door, crisp red flowers nestled in neat little boxes below the white-trimmed, wood-framed windows. As I opened the door, I was embraced by a tableau of smiling, laughing men and gentle women chatting in their lilting Irish brogues, sipping on frothy pints of Guinness. A roaring fire drenched the pub in a lambent glow as a golden harp cascaded softly on the tape system. I felt a tug of yearning and warmth that I knew was the voice of my ancestors. "Welcome home, son. Welcome home."

I approached the kindly looking white-bearded old man behind the bar as he lovingly caressed a glass of Guinness until the froth had stilled at just the perfect point, at just the perfect temperature. An artist, indeed.

"Hello, there. I wonder if you could help me."

He didn't look up, so intent was he on not ruining the perfection of his craft.

"We're running late and I have to phone the hotel up ahead to tell them we're still coming. We're from Canadian television. I wonder if I could use your phone for just a couple of minutes."

He stopped pouring. And in words I will forever remember when friends reminisce about the beauty, warmth, generosity, friendliness and literary elegance of stunning Ireland, he intoned a memorable soliloquy worthy of James Joyce: "No. We don't like foreigners 'round here. Fuck off."

I reposted with an Old Gaelic word I knew. It began with "c"—Cork—and then hurriedly rejoined my fellow farters in the car.

We finally made it to the country inn around 10:30. They didn't tell us to fuck off but asked if we'd like something to eat after our long journey. The Irish are very confusing. Then the owner invited us into his massive, long bar. At the end sat two men on stools. At first it was hard to tell if they were talking or singing, drunk or sober. Well, they were all four. What they were doing as they sipped on Guinness and Bushmills was taking turns at reading poems by William Butler Yeats. "The Magi," "Easter, 1916," "An Irish Airman Foresees His Death" and "Under Ben Bulben." Two men reading Yeats to each other at midnight, in between a Bushmills and a Guinness. This is the Ireland I prefer to remember.

7

Pleasantville

There are many ironies in the Irish conflict; one involved the guns. The Protestant Ulster Volunteer Force killed and bombed the IRA and civilians with weaponry given to them by Beirut Christians who had captured the armaments from the Palestinian Liberation Organization. The IRA's favorite weapon was the high-powered, American-made ArmaLite assault rifle. Their main supplier was the Great Socialist People's Libyan Arab Jamahiriya. Again, money and political influence, not religion, lay behind the revolutionary largesse.

Another Islamic country with a penchant for selling tons of guns is Iran. But both countries' weapons sales are minuscule on the global scale. "The Great Satan," as Iran calls the U.S., is by far the most prolific exporter of arms, accounting for 40 percent of the world's market. It will sell to almost anyone, including dictators and human rights abusers. Among its biggest customers are those bulwarks of democracy, Egypt and Saudi Arabia, and, of course, Israel. Egypt is 90 percent Sunni Muslim. Wahhabism, a fundamentalist form of the Sunni sect, dominates Saudi Arabia. Another unpleasant and "better forgotten" fact is that Osama bin Laden, most of the 9/11 hijackers, and their money came from Saudi Arabia. Iran is Shia and therefore an enemy.

Nevertheless, Islam is one of the three great monotheistic religions. Christianity and Judaism are the other two. It was founded by Mohammed around 600 CE and split into its two main sects after his death in a row over who should succeed him. From its birthplace in Saudi Arabia, Islam spread across the Mediterranean into the Holy Land. Christian armies launched a crusade, or Holy War (sound familiar?) to overthrow the Muslims and take back Jerusalem and its historic sites. They won and went on to attack Muslims and Jews in other countries in twelve more crusades. Any wonder when Muslims today hear the word "crusade," they think back to the violence of the Christian armies and wonder if it is happening all over again?

True Islam is a religion of wonder and deep theological insight, and it has received a very bad rap from Westerners. Yes, a relatively few Muslims have shot the religion and others in the foot and various body parts by behaving very badly. As in Christianity, zealous literalists, bigoted evangelists and ignorant "scholars" have corrupted it. As in Christianity, Islam has more champions for social justice and human rights than it does for fundamentalism and fanaticism. The fanatics are still the few, but as Western hostility toward Islam grows irrationally, so too will the ranks of its own crusaders. And just to remind ourselves of that overused but accurate political cliché, as long as the plight of the Palestinians remains unresolved, so too will the threat of more violent attacks on the West and its surrogate, Israel.

Until 1978, Iran was a surrogate state of the United States and the United Kingdom. Then came the good news and the bad news. The good news was that the oil-wallowing, self-proclaimed King of Kings, puppet Shah Muhammad Reza Pahlavi, his sybaritic excesses and his murderous secret police were gone. The bad news was his replacement, everybody's sweetheart, let's have a big hand for Salman Rushdie's greatest admirer, the one, the only, the king of comedy, Ayyyatollahh Khomeeeiiinnniii!"

"Good morning. We're from CTV. Canadian Television. We were told to come here for our press credentials."

"Have a seat, please. The secretary is busy at the moment."

Including the driver, we were five, which was appropriate since we worked for a current affairs program *W-Five*. But it was soon to become *W-Four* because Jim Reed, the correspondent, could stay in Teheran for just one day. Time for one piece to camera for a documentary we hadn't begun to shoot and had no idea what it should say. Jim had to zip back to Canada to do more pieces to camera for a story about a train. Serious stuff, television journalism.

"Can you tell us if the Secretary will be much longer? It's been an hour now and we've got a lot to do. Could we just go off and do a bit of filming and come back?"

"Filming? You want to do filming?"

"Yes, I told you we wcre from Canadian Television."

"But you didn't say you wanted to do filming. You have to go to the Ministry of Information for that."

"But this is the Ministry of Information."

"Yes. But not for filming."

Out into the sun that was cooking the city at a steady 33°C. Jet-lagged, hot, sweating, no credentials and no filming meant we were in excellent spirits. Which got even better when we met the right Secretary at the right Ministry. I don't know the Farsi word for him but in English it's "asshole!"

If you ever have to write him a letter, simply address it to: Fuckwit, Teheran. It will go straight to him.

Or even: Asshole, Iran. He will get it immediately. Even the insertion of the letter "r" to satisfy the *Oxford Dictionary*'s pedantry ("arsehole *n. coarse slang* 1 anus. 2 *offens.* contemptible person.") will not delay the missive a microsecond.

"Why do you come to Iran? You won't tell the truth. You work for the CIA. Why should I allow you to do anything? Where is your list?"

"List?"

"I must have a list of everything you want to film. You were told to bring a list."

"No, we weren't. But we wanted to ask your guidance on this." (A lie, of course, but we needed him more than he needed us.)

"No, you don't. You just want to tell lies."

What one wanted to reply was: "Listen, asshole, we didn't want to come to your appalling booze-banned country in the first place. You can take your fucking country and your Islamic revolution and shove them both up your pathetic rectum!" But that might have meant twenty in an Iranian slammer alongside human rights workers, other journalists and now, even bloggers.

Two hours later, with the credentials grudgingly issued, *W-Five* headed for a public park that would provide a neutral background for Jim's piece to camera so, like the words, it would be meaningless enough to fit anywhere in the documentary. Jim said something like: "Iran is at the crossroads and the Islamic Revolution may have a bumpy journey. The people of Iran and their ayatollah will determine just how bumpy in the months to come." Yeah, I know, and time will tell.

Then it was off to the airport for Jim. Lucky Jim.

Next day, Jimless, was an ADD. Another demo day. Having a mind like a steel trap, I thought that tens of thousands of them jammed into a square, shouting their praises to the ayatollah, might make good pictures.

The brief for the documentary was to explain what Islam and Khomeini meant in the new Iran. The best approach would be to tell the story through the eyes of an Iranian, someone who could articulate to a Western audience why, almost overnight, Iran had changed from a capitalist, Western-oriented country to a seemingly fanatical, fundamentalist Islamic state where everything and everyone Western were evil itself. And all *W-Five* had to do was to find the right person, who spoke English and who would agree to appear on Western television. There had been easier assignments.

The demonstration was due to start at two in the afternoon. It was an overcast but stifling day. The crowd, all men, began swarming into the square hours earlier. Again and again they would come up to us and yell. I wasn't sure what exactly they were saying, but it didn't appear they were inviting us home for tea; it rather sounded like they were telling us to get out of their country and never come back. Interspersed with the Farsi invective were a few shouts of "CIA" thrown in for good measure. For two days *W-Five* had been abused, heckled, shoved and threatened. Ubiquitous armed thugs, Islamic enforcers called Komitees, stopped us from filming every time we ventured into the streets. The heat was an unbearable 40°C, and no cold beer awaited us in the empty hotel fridge. I fixed that later by swapping a smuggled bottle of cognac for twenty-four Heinekens. Can't give away the source, as it were. Drink can kill, they say. Still, this is what we were paid to do. No need to grin, but certainly a duty to bear it. And on it went.

Then the last straw.

"You Americans, you are CIA. You should leave Iran. Go away! Go away!"

"Why don't you fuck right off!?" I reposted lightly.

The Iranian did as he was requested and dissolved into the crowd. What an asshole! And then it happened. My giant brain informed me that the guy I had emphatically told to disappear, and who had very effectively obeyed my order, was different. He had abused me *in English. He* was the documentary. Oooh, shit. Shit!

There had to be a hundred thousand in the square. The official estimate was one million. Whatever, there were a lot. Men with stirrup pumps strapped to their backs sprayed mists of cooling water over the surging masses, who roared fervent chants and swayed and bent and swayed and bent in a field of congealed devotion.

"The Imam is coming! The Imam is coming!"

He wasn't, but Iranian Air Force F14 Tomcat fighter jets screamed low overhead in spectacular celebration of the revolution. A couple of mullahs extolled the new Iran from a rickety stage and then, half an hour later, it was over. The crowd loosened and spread. And out popped the Iranian! The one I'd ever so politely told to remove himself. Groveling apologies weren't needed because he hadn't heard me. His abuse, he explained, was just his trying to be one of the boys.

His name was Majid Naini. A good-looking, thin guy in his mid-twenties who had been studying in the U.S. and was back in Teheran for a couple of months to see his family. He would be very happy to tell Canadians about Islam, the revolution and Khomeini, whom he called the savior of Iran. His dream was to kiss the Ayatollah's feet (huh?) but he knew it was just a dream. Despite his two years in Chicago, Majid seemed a genuinely devout Muslim who used materialism to pay for his education to fuel his soul.

Two days later, we went to Majid's house and set up the camera to film the family in prayer, reading from the Muslim Holy Book, the Koran, and eating a midday meal. As the camera rolled, there was a pounding on the door.

"Turn the camera off, please. Turn it off!" ordered Majid's father. One of his teenage daughters went to the door. Westerners have been seeing entering this house. Who are they? What business do they want with you? The girl showed the Komitee thugs our government press credentials and they left. Someone was watching us, not from above but from the ominous ground, probably the new secret police who used to be known as the shah's brutal SAVAK, trained in torture, terror and execution by the CIA and the Israeli Mossad. Iran was still a population of informers. They were too terrified not to be, either under the shah or Khomeini.

We had been a week in Iran and still had not sighted Khomeini, and Majid's dream remained just that. The only move to make was to gamble on a five-hour drive south to the holy city of Q'um, where Khomeini was reputed to live. We made a 6:00 AM start to beat the dust and airless suffocation of the desert. Stern local officials in Q'um did arrange for us to meet and interview a senior mullah and guaranteed us an oppor-tunity to film Khomeini later that afternoon. Oh, sure.

But Allah was indeed Akba that day in Q'um. Just after 2:00 PM, a huge convoy drew up to a school of learning where we were told the Ayatollah would preach to his pupils. He stepped out of a white Chevy 4x4 and walked slowly toward the camera without any interference from the dozens of security men. We' had been checked out and I guess we checked out. Cameraman Randy Platt walked backward so the Ayatollah's stare was always straight into the lens. Up a flight a stairs. Then the holiest of holy men stopped perhaps three feet in front of the lens; a brooding, menacing face, almost dazed. We were face to face with one of the most hated and most loved men on earth. Majid Naini instinctively stepped forward, went down on one knee and bowed his head. Ayatollah Khomeini offered his hand and Majid held it gently and kissed it. And Allah was in his soul that day in the Holy City of Q'um.

Back in Toronto, I structured the documentary, paper-assembled the picture sequences and interviews, wrote the script and gave it to Jim to voice. The film editor was a rotund genius who kept muttering that he didn't want to go to his daughter's wedding. Then, as always, the most dreaded moment in any producer's life, the screening for the bosses who would decide if the finished product was good enough to go to air on *W-Five*. The moment had come.

"A piece of shit," was the highest praise it got. "Re-cut it and rewrite it."

Allah may have blessed Majid Naini that day in the Holy City of Q'um, but he had stayed well clear of one *W-Five* producer.

8

Cruel Britannia

Politically isolated but bellicose, Iran needs all the friends it can get, and one of its newest, and most powerful, is India. In 2005 both countries caused some sphincter tightening by signing a deal that brought them closer together. The multi-billion-dollar agreement was not for nuclear technology. (Iran seems to be on the way to making the first "Shia Muslim bomb." Sunni Pakistan has its own, as do Christians of the U.S., U.K., France, plus the Jews, the Hindus, the godless Russians, the Taoist Chinese and who knows about the crazed North Koreans?) The deal was for a gas pipeline to run from Iran to India. It signaled a nexus between the enigmatic gun- and fighter-supplying Iran and India, as noted, a nuclear superpower in the region. India has come a long, long way.

Indian civilization has been around for over five thousand years. Its main religion is Hinduism, but it is also home to Sikhs, Jains, Zoroastrians, and is the world's third most populous Muslim country. Hindus believe what comes around goes around in a cycle of birth, life, death and rebirth until they are purged of sin and suffering and their God releases them into His presence.

A note about their sacred cows: Hindus don't worship the scrawny beast but they do honor it because it takes little and gives a lot. In fact, the cow caused a rebellion that could not have happened to a nicer group of colonizers. In the seventeenth century, the British East India Company began its cycle of depredation. It squeezed out the Portuguese, the Dutch and the French and established British dominance. One fine day in 1857, the sensitive British army told its Indian sepoys, or local soldiers, that their new bullets had been greased with cow fat. That started a rebellion that lasted a year, with nasty massacres (as opposed to quite attractive massacres) on both sides. The British army eventually won and then handed power to Her Britannic Majesty's government in London.

Today the British have a lot to answer for. Like a global vacuum cleaner, they sucked up everything they felt was rightfully theirs, which didn't leave much for anyone else: Australia, and damn the Abos; New Zealand, and damn the Maoris; much of Africa, and damn the Fuzzy Wuzzies; the entire North American continent where the incontinent British defecated on all from a great height; the Chinks, the Wogs, the Blackies, the Micks. *"Rule Britannia, marmalade and jam. Five Chinese crackers up your asshole. Bang, bang, bang, bang, bang."*

And just what did Britannia do for India? She taught the people subservience, obsequiousness and how to make a good gin and tonic when the sun went down. She also taught them how to write reports in triplicate. The British taught India the terrorism of bureaucracy.

→▸●◂←

His office was huge, tattered and somewhat bare. He, dapper and important.

Mr. Arif S. Khan
Official Spokesman
Ministry of External Affairs
Government of India

So began our "recky," the reconnaissance trip to set wheels in motion, to find an office and personal accommodation, to assess our professional requirements before coming back to establish the CBC's first permanent presence in India.

"We are very happy that the Canadian Broadcasting Corporation is coming to India to set up a bureau. My ministry will do all we can to help. You will, of course, have to receive accreditation. PIB (Press and Information) cards, journalists' visas, letters from your company, the names of your spouse and children. But these are formalities, really. Now, how can I help?"

"Well, Mr. Khan, we will be bringing a large amount of technical equipment both for radio and television. Can you advise us, because in the past I have had some problems bringing TV gear into India. For instance, will we have to pay duty?"

"Oh, don't worry about that, Mr. Scully. All press people who are setting up offices here receive a one-time-only duty-free exemption, so you can bring in all your packets (that's what Indians call everything bigger than a matchbox) without paying duty."

"That's great. Thanks. Can I have a letter to show Indian Customs at the airport when we come back next month with the equipment?"

"Of course. Now I have a meeting with the minister." At which, he got up and walked out.

Walking in were Mr. Venu and Mr. Sachdeva.

V.P. Sachdeva
Publicity Officer (PR)
External Publicity Division
XPR Section
Government of India
Ministry of External Affairs

"Mr. Khan says we'll be given a letter to show Indian Customs at Indira Gandhi International Airport (IGIA) when we come back with all our radio and TV equipment, and it'll say we have a one-time duty-free exemption."

"Yes, yes. That is quite correct. We do this for all correspondents," said Mr. Venu, Mr. Sachdeva's boss.

"Fine, thank you. When can we get the letter?"

"Come back tomorrow and it will be ready."

We had reached agreement at 10:30 AM that morning, and all they had to do was get it copied and signed. But this was India, so tomorrow it would have to be.

The letter:

18-10-94

To:

Asst. Collector of Customs

IGIA

New Delhi

Dear Sir,

Mr. John Scully, correspondent on behalf of

Canadian Broadcasting Corporation, has been posted in New Delhi for a period of three years. This is the first time the CBC is opening its office in New Delhi. In order to carry out their professional duties, Mr. Scully, on behalf of CBC, will be bringing the equipment attached below for official use.

It is requested that all assistance within the Customs rules (Transfer of Residence) may be extended to him.

Yours faithfully,
V.P. Sachdeva
Publicity Office (PR)

Appended was our long list of equipment. Cameras, recorders, monitors, microphones, cables and so on.

"Thank you, Mr. Sachdeva. Um, the letter doesn't mention the one-time duty-free exemption. Shouldn't that be in there?"

"No, no. This is the standard letter we give for Customs clearance. There will be no problem, I can assure you."

If you have ever been unlucky enough to get stuck behind a TV crew checking in at the airport, you will know how much gear they travel with. Add to this, personal baggage for a three-year stint and we had thirty-three cases, twenty-seven of which were equipment weighing a mere 388 kilograms.

My country's least favorite airline, Air Canada, was at its obliging best. No, we won't give you a break; your excess baggage fee will be $17,000. Gee, taa. Our alternative was to ship the gear as cargo, at a fraction of the cost, rather than as accompanied baggage on the same flight. TV crews hate doing this, though. Cargo goes to another building, requires different Customs clearance procedures, and there's also the risk of theft, of it being off-loaded or being sent in the opposite direction. But this time we took precautions. The CBC's London handling agent at Heathrow arranged a guarantee for it to be on the same flight, AC896 to Delhi, for $2,000, a saving to the CBC of $15,000.

Not that it mattered to me personally. It wasn't my money. But it would come out of the bureau budget, which was small enough to start with. Any big monetary hit would affect our ability to cover stories, so we tried to save every dime.

The flight from London to Delhi took the usual eight hours. Arrival time was 2:00 AM. Few international flights ever arrive or depart from Delhi at anything but the most miserable hours the night can bring. That's so ongoing passengers will arrive in Europe or Asia in daylight. On arrival, the first trick was to retrieve six personal bags, beat off pawing porters, taxi touts and moneychangers, and clear Customs. After Customs, more beating off of pawing porters, tugging kids, taxi touts and moneychangers. And then to bed.

Hotel The Claridges was a decaying monument to the Raj, superficially charming and deeply frayed. But at 4:30 AM it was heaven. A few hours' sleep, then the CBC's business manager, Davinder Gupta, and I would go back to the airport to pick up the gear.

India had already swamped me; the crushing millions of never-ending people, the chaos and insanity of the traffic, and the at least two dozen English-language newspapers. So let's not go back to the grubby old Customs shed for a few minutes, and instead take a look at my other new India.

→|=≡ ● ≡=|←

Monday, February 5, 1996, dawned smokingly in New Delhi. No different from any other. A bracing morning aglow with fetid pollution and pools of dung from both man and beast. The lads in the weather office were busy with their charts and wind machines, discernibly more active after a fiery lamb vindaloo. By 5:00 PM they had it sussed. Tomorrow, Tuesday, would start foggily. That was good enough for the boys and girls in the ops room of the domestic carrier, Indian Airlines. They immediately cancelled all flights scheduled to leave Delhi in the morning. Only problem was, Tuesday's dawn came bright and clear. You could see for miles. Why didn't the ops boys and girls wait until morning? One thing I learned in India is never ask why. Your brain will hurt.

With the dawn came the buses. Battered, filthy mechanical jokes, real killers. Jammed, crammed, slammed. There were three types: those run by the Delhi Municipal Corporation and two private companies. The Indy 500 was a pedal-car race compared with the Delhi buses as they hurtled down the pot-holed, cracked and crevassed roads, desperate to be first to pick up the prized passengers. The drivers clearly had learned their tactics from the kamikaze pilots of the Japanese Imperial Navy. The highest number of kills by far went to the Red Line buses. They were constantly crushing motor scooters, pedestrians, cars, goats, coconut vendors, the odd cripple, a couple of beggars, then home for tea.

The Red Line menace had become so bad, the burghers (probably vegetarians) of Delhi decided something had to be done. So they did it. They had a solution that verged on Einsteinian genius. They would paint all their buses blue! But this being India, nobody painted anything, and the buses never got their blue hue.

When a bus hits an object in India, usually human, the passengers conduct a ritual as old as the civilization (or lack of it) itself. Off they get, find a few rocks or pipes or anything that could be classed as rubble, which means virtually the entire old city, and pelt the bus, break its windows and then set it on fire. Now they cannot get to work, but they have demonstrated admirable public spirit.

While all this was happening, in the parlance of the Indian newspapers, the driver "is absconding." Even if it happened three days ago, he is still absconding. With good reason. If the crowd didn't belt him senseless, then Delhi's finest police officers would.

In mid-1995, I saw a spectacular ritual performance, a real class act. A Red Line bus had run over a motor scooter. Off jumped the crowd. Down rained the rocks. Up licked the flames. Only problem was, they had forgotten about the rider trapped under the bus. Most unfortunate. Burned to a crisp.

The *Times of India* crusaded for bus safety. Here's a story from April 13, 1996.

> An anonymous caller rang the city police complaint cell last week. His complaint: a traffic policeman was taking money from private bus drivers at the Kamla Market intersection.

Next morning, the traffic department swung into action with assistant commissioner of police, Prem Nath, clad in plainclothes, reaching the spot in an auto-rickshaw. And the police was [sic] caught red-handed with Rs1,400 ($us50).

After policing "reckless" Red Line and Blue Line buses and "errant" motorists, the traffic police is [sic] now policing its own personnel. Or so it seems, after the initiation of departmental inquiries against eight inspectors, 33 sub-inspectors and assistant sub-inspector and as many as 96 constables in the last three months ... Just over 1,800 men and women were transferred out ... and how is the traffic department filling up the vacancies? It may sound strange but it wants constables six feet in height.

"Height imparts visibility at clogged intersections," the CP explained.

Added *The Indian Express*:

The police crackdown has resulted in an appreciable drop in the number of fatalities involving Red Line and Blue Line buses. Against 11 deaths in February, there were only five deaths in the month of March, the police said.

Indian has an extraordinary sixty thousand registered newspapers. Here is a sample of some English headlines:

"Five Elephants Arrested At City Limits."

"Woman's Body Goes On Rampage."

"King Hussein To Visit Jordan."

"Planet Named After Chinaman."

We were still on page one, and still had to retrieve our gear from Customs. The morning was a surprisingly brisk 14°C. In a few hours that would soar to the high 30s. The driver of our aging white Contessa, Hindustan Motors' version of the British Vauxhall Victor, was Om. That's it. Om. A pleasant, always smiling, helpful young guy from Nepal. But he was just a driver, so you were permitted to cuff him round the head if he drove too fast, too slow or at the right speed. Indians like to cuff their drivers every now and then. Twice a day is the recommended rate. Keeps them in their place. You can also belt them for stopping too near a puddle, not opening the door fast enough or letting you carry anything heavier than an envelope. Getting lost, or falling asleep at 2:00 AM while waiting for Sir to finish the Chivas Regal, well, both of those are, of course, capital, not cuffable offenses.

Om was about to get his first cuff of the day. He had wandered away from the Contessa to talk to some of his mates in the car park. So when Davinder and I walked up to the car, we found we were Omless. No big deal. He'd be around somewhere. Davinder spotted him first. Ouch! Ow! To be fair, Om wasn't physically belted, just verbally, and so, after a good tongue-lashing, we were off to the airport to get the gear.

Nothing to this, we thought. After we get the gear, we'll find apartments, get a post office box and finally start acting like real journalists doing real stories. What could be simpler?

New York International Film and TV Festival — Silver Medal, Best Documentary.
L to R: Keith Morrison, reporter, and wife; Lionel Lumb, executive producer;
John Scully, producer.

With reporter Peter Trueman taking a break in Bulawayo, Zimbabwe.

In the bush during civil war in Rhodesia.
L to R: Keith Bushnell, camera; Scully; Michael Sullivan, BBC reporter.

Meeting an armed farmer during civil war in Rhodesia. L to R: Michael Sullivan,
BBC reporter; farmer with gun; Keith Bushnell, camera; John Scully, producer.

Playing director on a balcony of the hotel in Kampala, Uganda.

Last days of the Vietnam War.
L to R: Peter Trueman, reporter; Walter Corbett, camera; Scully, producer.

Near Kuala Lumpur, Malaysia. Scully and cameraman Brian Kelly.

Great Wall of China.

Confronting the smell of death, Beirut.

With Phalange Christian militia fighter, Beirut.

On research break, Rabat, Morocco.

Boarding a plane for Jonestown, Guyana.

Scully's unlikeliest pose, Jamaica.

With a boat person in a refugee camp, Malaysia.

Getting set for an on-camera, with cameraman Jean-Guy Nault, Kyoto, Japan.

Preparing a shot for a documentary, Toronto International Airport.

On a barge down the Rio Coco, bordering Honduras and Nicaragua.
On left: Bruce Garvey, reporter; Michael Savoie, camera. On right: Scully, producer;
Macello Montecino, associate producer.

CBC Journal crew, Kampala, Uganda. L to R: Ann Medina, reporter; Michael Sweeney,
camera; Henry Gombya, associate producer; Alister Bell, sound; Scully, producer.

A quieter moment during an uprising in Chile.
L to R: Scully, producer; Russ Froese, reporter; Jean-Guy Nault, camera.

On the Yangtze River, China, with reporter Rae Corelli.

Stranded in the Sahara Desert, Mali, with reporter Ann Medina.

25th anniversary of CBC *The Journal* 2007.
L to R: Sully; former reporter Russ Froese; soundman Alister Bell.

Daughter's wedding, 2004.
Back: John and Toni Scully. Front: Chris Staig and Emma Scully.

Father and son Jerome, 2008.

PRESS INFORMATION BUREAU
GOVT. OF INDIA

PRESS
CORRESPONDENT
TEMPORARY

JOHN P. SCULLY
Cable Public Affairs
Canadian Channel, Canada

105

DATE OF ISSUE :
VALID UPTO : 2-9-1997

Principal Information Officer

Specials

B.B.C. CLUB (BELFAST) 1971

INSERT CARD KEY HERE™

MEMBER'S NAME New Room B/lt

Supplied by E. A. CLARE & SON
LIVERPOOL L.33DW
Tel. No. 051 207 1336

CBC TV NEWS

NOM/NUM
JOHN P. SCULLY
SIGNATURE
S.I.N./N.ASS. SOCIALE

NATIONAL T.V. NEWS
ACCREDITED REPRESENTATIVE / REPRÉSENTANT AUTORISÉ

NEWS EDITOR

Accreditations and Press Cards

First stop, the Jor Bagh Post Office in South Delhi. Letters strewn over the ground, on the steps, everywhere but where they should be in customers' post boxes. Which is what we are trying to get. A post office box. Lots of men sitting at ancient desks are working very hard at reading the newspaper. Ask one of them a question and he employs the age-old Indian bureaucratic tactic of pretending not to hear you, hoping you'll go away. When this ruse fails, he gets very agitated and grunts that you must see his supervisor. Where is he? He's out. When will he be back? I don't know. Go away. Well, who is his deputy? He's the fellow who sits there, as he points to a stark desk devoid of paper or man. Only a phone, and it's ringing. Is the deputy not here today? Yes, he's here. Where? Outside. Why? Because his phone keeps ringing.

We finally got a post office box, but the mail we received was not always what we expected. Twice, we opened the box to find someone's lunch. Maybe he sorted the *samosas*, ate the letters and posted his *pakoras*. Who knows?

When trying to rent an apartment in Delhi, with cash (two years in advance, half of it under the table to cut the landlord's tax bill), Dick Gordon and I had to prove we were who we said we were: Canadians representing the CBC. Passports, press credentials, official letters from the Indian government were insufficient. The landlord wanted more. Another letter! Two, in fact. One, signed by the CBC heavies in Toronto, saying yes, indeed, these two good-looking lads are bona fide employees of the CBC, wasn't good enough. How do I know the CBC really exists? I want a letter from the "president" of Canada attesting to the existence of the Canadian Broadcasting Corporation, together with a copy of its charter and a list of all of its board members. All this to rent an apartment. With cash. Up front. And underneath.

My brain hurts. Or at least I thought it did until I came across "Project Tiger."

Project Tiger is India's attempt to save the Bengal tiger from extinction. It is much sought after for its bones and skin. The skin for the floors, the bones for the whores, to satisfy the demands of Asia's sexually challenged. In 1995 Project Tiger began a census of the tiger population in India's national parks. To videotape this event required the permission of the project's boss, Mr. Arin Gosh.

"Yes, that should be no problem, Mr. Scully. I will have to write a letter to the Chief Warden of Rajasthan, Mr. R.S. Bhandari, for his permission. So I'll need a letter."

"Um, I'm not quite sure what you mean. Do you mean you will write a letter asking permission for the CBC to film the tiger census?"

"Yes. But first I need a letter."

"From whom?"

"From you."

"From me?"

"Yes."

"Why?"

"I have to have a letter from you officially asking me to write a letter to the chief ranger. And you will have to get a letter from the Ministry of External Affairs, Protocol Division, making the request for your filming permission. And that should be addressed to the Chief Wild Life Ranger in Rajasthan."

At the government press office I was asked frequently to write a letter saying I wanted them to write a letter. The reason being, the party to whom the second letter is being sent cannot blame the second party for the contents of the first letter because it was requested by another party—the first party. Me.

It can't get any sillier, can it? Oh, well, let's go back to the airport and find out.

"Hello. I've come to collect a shipment. It arrived on Air Canada last night and here's a letter from the Indian government allowing me to bring it into the country duty free."

I was talking to two men seated as a desk inside the Indian Customs storage shed. Shed is a slight misnomer. The facility was the size of four jumbo jet hangars, vast tiers stacked to the roof with goods yet to be cleared by Customs. Clearly, the owners of the goods did not have a letter from Mr. L.K. Sachdeva. A few minutes earlier, we had been stopped at the main entrance to the Customs area, the parking lot.

Official in cap: "Passport. Purpose of visit. Address. Vehicle registration number. Now take this form over to the guard box," which was all of four meters away.

Guard with another form: "Passport. Purpose of visit. Time of entry."

"So now we can drive our vehicle into the car park?"

"No. You must have a special pass. You get it from the officer over there who gave you the first form."

"But I've just filled in two forms. You've also got my passport and the vehicle details. Isn't that enough?"

"No. You must have a pass for the vehicle."

"Why didn't he give me one?'

"Because you didn't ask for one."

"But …"

But then they closed for lunch, so we had no pass. The CBC

car and the truck we had hired to transport the gear were left on the side of the road, outside the gate. But the best was yet to come.

"Stop! Where is your pass?"

The inquisitor this time was an old khaki-uniformed guard armed to his brown-stained teeth with a World War I vintage rifle. Neither it nor its owner had probably ever gone "bang" in their entire lives and seemed highly unlikely to do so now.

"Pass? What pass? You mean these forms I filled in at the main gate?"

"No. They are no good. You must have permission to enter the Customs shed. Do you have permission?"

"I have this letter from the Indian government saying I can come to the airport and collect my goods duty free."

"No. This is no good. You have to have a letter from the proper authority. Do you have such a letter?"

"Who is the proper authority? Isn't this letter from the Indian government authority enough? I mean, it's from your government, allowing a member of the foreign press to enter the Customs area to collect equipment. That is what this letter means!"

About now, the jet lag hit. I wanted to lie down and go to sleep and make it all go away. But that was impossible. I didn't have a letter from the proper authority.

Just then, an old school friend of Davinder called out a greeting: "Hey, you old poofter!" At least, that's what the Hindi sounded like. "Hello, you silly little wanker," was the possible retort.

"John, this is very good. My friend is the head of security at Customs. Would you like to see your equipment?"

And there it was, three tiers up. I spotted the camera case, the tripod tube, boxes of tapes. All nineteen pieces.

"Great. Can I take them now?" I asked the security boss.

"No, Mr. John, but I will take you to see the superintendent. He's a very good friend of mine. He will fix everything."

This sounded promising.

"And, please, Mr. John, don't worry. Please."

The superintendent's door was closed and had no glass panels to see through.

Outside seethed a line of hot, disheveled brokers, shippers and supplicants, all waiting their turn for the superintendent's magic rubber stamp.

"Damn. This is going to take hours, Davinder."

"No, no, Mr. John," interjected the security man. "Just go in." Translated, that means you are a white foreigner. You are better than them. They will not say anything. The class system is still functioning well in India. Go in.

→──• ◦─←

There's another system functioning in India, the real India, you could argue—the villages, far away in time and reality. Eighty percent of India's population (1.1 billion est. 2006) is rural; half a billion (yes, billion) are illiterate, and most of them are hungry. They make their houses of mud and dung; buffalo are their tractors; sewage is their drinking water. For every one thousand babies born, fifty-four die. In Canada that number is five. And the number is also five for the number of Indians who have AIDS— five million, although India and some U.N. workers insist the figure is much lower. Twenty-first century messages of hygiene and health are still lost in a babble of eighteen official languages, two hundred unofficial "mother tongues" and a thousand dialects. Many have no idea who is their prime minister. Some still vote for Indira Gandhi. She was assassinated in 1984.

In a remote village an hour's pitch and yawl in a Jeep from the city of Lucknow, I saw the Uttar Pradesh authorities bravely begin trying to educate its poverty-burdened inhabitants about polio: how to prevent it with a proper course of vaccination and, if diagnosed early enough, how it could be treated and even cured. India has the highest polio numbers in the world, despite the Salk vaccine.

But polio crusader Dr. B.B. Brigita might well have come from the moon. It didn't help that her pager went "beep!" every few minutes. And every time she checked, there was an emergency. India was in deep trouble in a vital cricket match in Calcutta. The polio campaign didn't have a chance in this village. Folks were too busy trying to avoid starvation to keep track of dates for follow-up vaccinations. They couldn't afford to lose a day's work in the fields or pay the bus fare to take a sick kid to a hospital seventy kilometers away. So, the babies got sick and died. Others survived as harsh jokes. One ten-year-old girl scuttled across the dusty yard on her backside and her hands. Her legs were of no use. They were bent up beside her head like a two-clawed lobster. Still, she was lucky, maybe. Unlike many other girls, deformed or not, curiously, she was not killed at birth; one study reckons twenty million female fetuses have been aborted in India in the last two decades. Girls mean dowry. Girls cost money. Boys don't.

While Dr. Brigita was tiptoeing across the rivulets of sewage snaking through the village, she suddenly stopped. A beturbanned, grinning man was making quite silly gurgling and hiccupping noises while pouring water on a younger man's arm. The younger man was whistling with pain, sucking in air and panting. A scorpion had bitten him on the middle finger of his right hand. The man making the silly noises was the village quack. His cure was to pour cold water on the victim's arm, muttering and jabbering all the while. Then he rubbed a magic potion on the fiery bite.

(Note on scorpions: About fifty of their 1,500 species are not to be messed with. The sting can cause severe skin reactions, neurological, respiratory and cardiovascular collapse. Death, in other words. Scorpions use their pincers to grasp their prey, arch their tail over their body to drive in their stinger to inject their venom, sometimes more than once. The good news? In general, scorpions are not aggressive. They do not hunt for prey; they wait for it. Scorpions are nocturnal and hide in crevices and burrows during the day to avoid the light. Accidental human stinging often occurs when scorpions are touched while in their hiding places, with most of the stings occurring on the hands and feet. [Scorpion information from e*Medicine.com*.] Remember that next time you are putting your shoes on. Socks, too.)

Our hard-bitten hero was barefoot, and who knows where he'd put his ungloved digit? No one seemed to know or care how he got bitten. Happened all the time. So, as I was saying before the scorpion sidetracked us, the local quack was rubbing his magic potion into the poor guy's bloated finger that was getting bigger and redder by the minute. Since nobody in the village could read, the quack had little fear of an inquiry from his local college of physicians and surgeons. His unguent on this hot, dusty day was a thick, browny-yellow ointment that came from a small can. In English it read: "Bicycle grease. Finest quality." Did it work? Both men were still upright when we left. But Dr. Brigita opined the bitten man would be dead by morning.

⤙ ● ⤚

Back to the very convenient class system and the airport. The superintendent was a hefty, middle-aged sari-clad woman with stripes of office on her shoulders. I suspect she had no idea who the security man was. Even so, she interrupted her conversation with a supplicant and turned to little, white me.

"I'm from Canada … blah, blah, blah."

"Yes. I see. But first I need to see documentation from the airline."

"Okay. It's right here in my briefcase. There we are."

"Yes, yes. Very good. Very good. Well, everything seems to be in order, Mr. Scully."

At last, the right person. Friendly, too. We were almost home.

"So can I collect the equipment now?"

"Not yet. First, you must get an official document called a Bill of Lading."

And where did I get that? Across a wasteland of scrub, garbage, urine and that other stuff, and into a decrepit, tired, shambling, large old wooden shack. Inside, a bureaucrat's dream. Four rows of men sitting at ancient upright typewriters, doing absolutely nothing. A scratch here, a fart there, a newspaper page turned somewhere else. This squadron of immobility had seen hot, frustrated Westerners stumble into their midst and turn bright pink with frustration right before their amused eyes many times. I was just one more. But Davinder was sensing that this Westerner was about to erupt. Perhaps the increasing use of the phrase "this is fucking unbelievable" was his biggest hint. Almost on his knees, Davinder pleaded, cajoled and begged with fistfuls of money for one of them to give us a blank Bill of Entry for Consumption, an extraordinary document eighteen inches wide and fifteen inches deep. We had to fill it out in ballpoint; then it had to be typed, not in duplicate, not in triplicate, not in quadruplicate, but in quintuplicate. Peck, peck, peck. One letter at a time. Value of equipment. Peck. Peck. Peck. Country of Consignment. Peck. Peck. Peck. Consignee's mother's maiden name. Peck. Peck. Peck. Time of paternal grandfather's last bowel movement. Peck. Peck. Peck.

At 3:30 PM: "Where do we take this?"

To the assistant collector of Customs, in another, much spiffier building over a kilometer away. Another brisk walk in the 35-degree sun. Mr. Assistant Collector of Customs was in a crisp, white, navy-styled uniform with epaulettes and lots of gold stripes and ribbons.

"First, you have to register the Bill of Entry," in the next office, that turned out to be a large common room, very common, with about twenty Customs brokers, shippers and runners (messenger "boys") all sweating and pouring over even thicker and more unwieldy documents. That was one-half of the room. On the other side, separated by a sturdy wooden railing, were the hard-working clerks, chatting to each other, calling for more tea, reading the paper, completely indifferent to the six or so brokers leaning over the railing, pleading for attention.

"Go, John. Push in ahead of them." And the white man won again.

"Could you register this, please?" I asked a very uncivil servant. Thirtyish. White unbuttoned shirt. Small mustache. He glanced over it and nonchalantly tossed it back.

"This is no good. You'll have to get a new one." And he simply turned and walked away.

"Excuse me! Hello!"

"What?"

"What's wrong with this?"

"You haven't filled out this line."

"I didn't type it out. A man at the Bill of Entry office did it."

"Well, it's no good. He'll have to type a new one on Monday."

"On Monday? But this is only Friday!"

"Yes, but it's four o'clock and they will be closed now. They don't work on Saturdays."

Time to tell a lie.

"Well, you should know that the prime minister is going to be very mad at you, personally. We have an interview with him tomorrow morning, so we must have the equipment tonight. I'm afraid I'll have to tell him exactly what happened here. And I'll make sure he has your name in writing."

"Okay, mister, please sit down and wait."

"How long will it take to get the bill registered?"

"Half an hour. Then you take it back to the assistant collector."

"What time does the assistant collector go home?"

"Five o'clock."

And he walked off for some more tea and chat with his fellow procrastinators. At ten to five I yelled out another "Hello!" He looked up, scribbled something in a book, stamped our document, flipped it back to me, and walked away. That consumed all of forty-five seconds of his time.

Finally: "Hello, sir. I'm back. Everything is registered."

"Let me see your documents."

Five to five.

"Yes, I see. And you say you have registered this with the proper authority next door?"

"Yes. See. It's stamped, dated and in proper order."

"I see."

He began to write down a list of figures on a lined sheet of paper.

"Excuse me, sir, I have a letter here from the Indian government giving me permission to use a one-time duty-free exemption for the camera gear. Here it is."

"This doesn't say anything about an exemption. Even if it did, you would still have to pay duty. There is no exemption for foreign journalists."

"I'm sorry, but there is. That is what this letter means!"

"No, it doesn't. There is no duty-free exemption for you."

"But there *has* to be. Your colleagues at the ministry didn't make this up!"

"There is no duty-free exemption."

"How much duty would I have to pay?"

"One hundred and ten thousand United States dollars."

"What? A hundred and ten thousand U.S. dollars? That's more than the equipment is worth! This is crazy! Would you please telephone Mr. Sachdeva? Here's his number."

Two minutes to five.

Mr. Sachdeva was still at his desk. "Ah, Mr. Scully. How are you? When did you arrive?"

"Last night. Look, we're having a problem getting our equipment released free of duty. I'm at the airport now. Could you please talk with the officer? He's Mr. Singh, the assistant collector of Customs."

"Certainly, Mr. Scully. Namaste, Shri Singh ..."

"Mr. Scully? Mr. Sachdeva here again. I've spoken with Mr. Singh and I think you should come to my office."

"Now?"

"Oh, no, Mr. Scully. Come on Monday. But don't worry, Mr. Scully. It will be all arranged."

I actually believed him.

At the end of this particular Friday, November 12, 1994, I counted the number of steps I had taken to try to get the gear released. My toes came in handy. It had been a long day. Gearless, but not Omless, we trudged back to the Hotel The Claridges. A stash of Heineken took a pounding that night and the pain eased, as my second Indian dawn was about to beckon.

Monday.

"Good morning, Mr. Scully. Sorry about the confusion and trouble on Friday. But I've checked with Mr. Venu and here's what you should do. Get your bureau to write a letter to us requesting clearance of your goods duty free."

"Sure. But we already have your letter."

"Yes, I know. But Indian bureaucracy, you know," he laughed.

Reporter Dick Gordon and I wrote a polite, detailed letter requesting the release of the equipment free of duty.

"Thank you, Mr. Scully. This will do fine. Now Mr. Gosh will write a letter to Customs and you will have your equipment free of duty. I'm sorry for all your problems. If there's anything more I can do to help, please feel free to call on me."

"Thank you, Mr. Sachdeva. When will the new letter be ready?"

"Tomorrow." Of course.

Mr. Gosh? New to me.

Letter:

The Asst Collector of Customs

IGIA

New Delhi

Sir,

The Canadian Broadcasting Corporation has opened their bureau in India and has posted Mr. Dick Gordon as Chief of Bureau and Mr. John Scully, correspondent New Delhi, and they have already been granted accreditation on behalf of the above organisation at the Govt. of India headquarters. For the news coverage by their New Delhi bureau, Canadian B'Casting Corporation have sent professional equipment which have already been arrived last week.

The equipment being imported will remain the property of the CBC in India and will not be sold or disposed of otherwise.

Customs authorities are therefore requested to expedite the clearance of professional equipment brought in by the correspondents of CBC under existing rules in this regard, subject to completion of formalities, if any.

Yours faithfully,

Swagata Gosh

(Dy. Principal Information Officer)

"But it still doesn't say anything about the goods being free of duty. It's the same letter written another way!" I protested.

"No, this one is different," barked:

Mr. C.R. Lekhra

Section Officer

Press Information Bureau

Govt of India

"A" Wing, Shastri Bhavan

New Delhi 110–001

A truly unhelpful man who was weeks away from retirement. We were being passed up the chain and down the chain at the same time. Neat trick.

And so, back at the cargo depot:

"This is the same letter you brought me last week! You are going to have to pay $110,000 in duty. That's it."

"What about if I gave you my own written personal guarantee. Would that help?"

Straws for the grasping didn't grow well at IGIA.

"It might help, Mr. Scully. Why don't you write me a personal guarantee?"

DECLARATION

This is to certify that we the Canadian Broadcasting Corporation have opened a bureau in India ... It is further declared ... not for sale ... use for CBC only ... will be returned to Canada.

John Scully

CBC

Correspondent

Tuesday morning. Ha! Did it work? Ha!

"Mr. Venu, this is getting absurd. You told me we have a duty-free exemption. You wrote this letter. But it doesn't work! Customs say we are entitled to *no* exemptions."

"Well, Mr. Scully, the letter is just to ease the bureaucracy. To be helpful. Of course, we cannot guarantee what Customs will do. You must understand that we are different arms of government."

"But the letter. I asked you why it didn't refer to exemptions and you said it didn't need to."

"That is quite correct. But if Customs don't accept it, I'm afraid it's out of our hands."

"Mr. Venu, we are talking a huge sum of money! One hundred and ten thousand U.S. dollars!"

"Yes, yes, I understand your concern. But I think you should see the Ministry of Finance."

"The Ministry of Finance? Why?"

"They are the ones who settle disputes of this nature."

"You mean I have to start all over again?"

"Yes, yes. It's better that way."

And no one can be blamed. An ingenious system of which the British could be rightly proud.

> To:
> Mr. R.P. Ramanan
> Jt. Secy of Customs
> Min of Finance
> New Delhi
>
> Sir
>
> The CBC ... led to believe their equipment would be allowed in free of duty ... guarantee not to sell or dispose of it ... And also enclosed is a list of the equipment with its as-new value, although most if it is used and would not be worth more than 30% of the value shown.
>
> John Scully, etc.

I was in deep shit. Although I had already undervalued the equipment in the original declaration (producers the world over do this when declaring highly expensive TV gear in duty-hungry developing countries, but I strongly advise them not to try it at places of landing like, say, Heathrow, or JFK or Toronto, unless they enjoy fraud trials), I was still looking at that $110,000. It was time to get some real muscle. Canada's high commissioner was new to the post and eager to make his mark. He promised he would take this matter to the very top. This was no way to treat Canada's national broadcaster. And he also gave me the services of the commission's own Customs shipper, who added weight to my now twice-daily visitations upon the shabby waiting rooms of the Ministry of Finance.

The Bible says God made the entire world, including India, in seven days. Very impressive. Nice one. But couldn't He have left out this fucking place? Coincidentally, seven other days had passed since the Canadian intervention. Seven days. That's 168 hours. Or 10,080 fucking minutes. Or 604,800 fucking seconds. Mr. Scully was getting impatient. Silly man. On November 25, 1994, one Vinay Chabray, Deputy Secretary (Customs) of whom I'd never heard or met in my fourteen trips to the Ministry of Finance, wrote me a lovely letter.

> Your request has been carefully examined and it is regretted that it cannot be acceded to. The accredited news agencies are already eligible for a concessional rate of Customs duty of 25% ad valorem. No further concessions are possible.

As Shakespeare put it in one of his finest works: "You're fucked, mate."

I added up the different steps I'd taken so far, including letters, faxes and phone calls. Eighty-two. And still gearless. And still looking at $110,000 duty, the equivalent of at least two trips to Kashmir, two to Sri Lanka and a couple to Pakistan. And I had another problem. I had already registered the Bill of Entry with

Customs, which meant I couldn't lower the value of the goods I had declared. Indian law forbade the submission of a second document in case someone (like me) wanted to change the declared value and pay less duty. What to do? What to do?

We discussed bribery. And if we chose to bribe the only honest person on duty? No gear for the CBC and the slammer for me. I take back what I said about God and India because God also invented Saturdays, and on Saturdays Indian Customs puts in a deputy to act as assistant collectors of Customs. This deputy, a gentle Sikh, was saddened by the story I told him. This was no way to treat guests in his country and he understood how the value of the equipment was inaccurate because I had been given improper advice. Of course, it was far less than on the original Bill of Entry. He had the authority to amend earlier declarations, which, as my sphincter realigned itself from my throat, he did, and from owing $110,000, we got away with $10,000.

From the time he signed the release document that brilliant Saturday morning in lovely south Delhi, it took another three full days to acquire the necessary signatures to finally release the gear. How many extra signatures did I end up needing? Twenty.

9

The Glamour, The Clamor

few years earlier, I was right next door in Bangladesh, making a documentary for the BBC about the victims of the great cholera plague. Tens of thousands were waiting for space so they could lie down and die, as vultures cawed and squawked over them. A million refugees were fleeing massacres and butchery in what was then East Pakistan. Teeming columns of the dying, collapsing in front of our BBC camera. A dog gnawed at the head of what could have been a man or a woman or a child. The grave was too shallow, the land too hard.

In a nearby city, we filmed a truck making its macabre morning rounds.

"Bring out your dead. Bring out your dead."

Two streets later and the truck was already overladen, arms flopping over the sides, bodies piled on top of bodies. Still, this was how it was in the great cholera plague. You died or you found a way to make a living. With a mountain of corpses as a backdrop, the driver and his helper posed for Bernard Hesketh's camera. They waved into the lens with big, bright smiles. No grim reapers here.

Bangladesh has a population of around 150 million, the eighth highest in the world. It is the same size as the U.S. state of Iowa. Iowa's population is three million. The capital of Bangladesh is Dhaka, perhaps the most densely populated city on the planet.

Babies are born on the street and many die on the street. Their mothers sit beside the motionless ragged bundles and hold out their hands for burial money. I saw a fetus lying in the gutter.

And then there was the Wrigley man. Tap, tap, tap on the car window. At first I saw a head but it had no ears. Then I realized he had no torso, either. He resembled a strip of chewing gum that had a head and a pair of flippers. And he was begging for mercy.

The terrorism of famine, flood, typhoons, plague, disease, hunger and poverty are Bangladesh's constant companions. The country used to be called East Pakistan. But before that it had been part of India, until the British drew their absurd maps that, in 1947, resulted in the atrocities and pogroms of Partition. Two Muslim Pakistans, East and West (now Pakistan), were separated by over 1,500 kilometers. India and Pakistan went to war twice after that. Bangladesh was created after a third war in 1971. It was a harrowing birth, with a Muslim majority and a Bengali Hindu minority. They hacked and chopped each other to death and, with tears and cries, they begged each other for deliverance.

A BBC TV crew witnessed one massacre. As reporter Tom Mangold narrated, ten Hindu men were rounded up and dragged into a city square. First, one was slapped in the face. Then another. The next sequence showed the Muslim men kicking the Hindus, who were wailing and begging them to stop. But they didn't. The machetes and knives began slicing and chopping the Hindus, who fell dying but not dead. The sun burned down as they writhed as if trapped in a slow-motion nightmare. Death would not be swift this day. Blood oozed from the wounds and the Hindus gurgled from their throats. The moaning ceased only when their God's mercy delivered them to the rattle of death.

As the war intensified, the city was cut off from the rest of the universe. No phones, no planes, just the intermittent telex message. (Telex was like an electronic typewriter whose messages were sent on wires around the world.) A BBC team was trapped in the Intercontinental Hotel along with other international media, often taking cover from the bombs in the hotel basement, but also shooting some of the war's most brutal film. Producer Lionel Lumb, reporter John Humphrys, cameraman Keith Skinner and soundman Ted Stoddard were doing a remarkable, even heroic job. There was just one problem. They had no way of getting their film to London, so the film was, in reality, useless.

Then, as Lumb tells it: "John Humphrys and I met with an old *koi hai*—a British expatriate and long-time riverboat captain who, we thought, might find us a boat and smuggle the film out to India through the river system. A hazardous venture that in retrospect I'm glad never came about. The Pakistan army was shooting at anything that moved in case it was carrying mujahadeen forces or arms. Then a Brit journalist arranged a plane to fly his and everyone's film out to the West through Burma. I was the lone voice that said the Burmese government was unpredictable and unreliable. There was a vote and I lost. Turns out I was right. The whole shebang (all networks' footage, including European) was impounded and not released until several months after the war.

"When our film finally got to London, I was further chagrined when the editor of that night's BBC *News* decided to run a miserly two or three minutes. And we had the best footage. ITV ran about six or eight minutes. But I became the hero of the networks and smuggled everyone's later film out on the night of the surrender and enjoyed a solo Lear jet flight for part of the journey to London."

The first prime minister of Bangladesh was Sheikh Mujibur Rahman, the boss of the political Awami League. Five years after his swearing in, Bangladesh suffered yet another catastrophe— famine—and the Sheikh appealed to the world for urgent food aid.

The international relief agency, World Vision, was one of the first charities to respond. Its people were organizing an airlift of as much rice as could be crammed into a stretch DC8 freighter. The DC8 was one of the early passenger jets, but when the wide-bodied planes came along, the DC8 was consigned to carrying freight, apart from a few of those I'll-never-fly-with-that-airline airlines. World Vision's DC8 was chartered from a company in Oakland, California, and Global Television had been invited to sit amid sacks of rice for the twenty-four-hour flight to Dhaka. First we had to get to Oakland. We were just about to leave the news-room for Toronto Airport when the phone rang.

"It's World Vision here. Listen, can any of you boys fly a DC8?"

Well, Reg Thomas could shoot film and David Studer could talk into a microphone and I, the senior field producer, was skilled at do-it-yourself lobotomies, but fly a DC8? Well, not today, but maybe by next week.

World Vision had hired the plane with one pilot, but regula-tions stated there had to be two pilots on a flight lasting twenty-four hours, including a refueling stop. Good thinking! But finding a second pilot was proving difficult. Global's news chief, Bill Cunningham, decided to scrap the DC8 plan, but he still wanted us to get to Bangladesh in a hurry. So we flew Air Canada to London, connecting to a Bangladesh Biman Airlines flight to Dakha.

"You're flying Biman?" sniggered the woman at the BA check-in desk at Heathrow. BA was Biman's handling agent. "Why don't you wait until tomorrow? We've got a flight to Dakha then."

But travel Biman we did. She was right; we should have waited.

The plane was a crumpled old Boeing 707, a sister of the DC8. Bits were flaking off the ceiling, and the seats were ragged, unhappy and very, very cramped. At midnight we touched down for refueling in steamy Bahrain, but if they were only refueling, why did they ask the passengers to leave the plane and take all of their belongings with them? All of our personal belongings? You mean my fridge? My washing machine? My car? My Spike Jones records? The furnace? Surely they didn't mean all of our personal belongings? No. Asshole.

"How long is the stop here?"

"We don't know."

"You don't know?"

"You see, this is Biman's only plane, and Sheikh Mujibur needs it for a trip to Africa."

"When?"

"Tonight."

"Tonight?"

"Tonight."

"And when will we have our plane back?"

"We really don't know, but it shouldn't be more than a few days."

"A few days? You must be joking!"

Nope, no joke.

So, all two hundred Bangladeshis and three Canadian lads filed into the waiting area at Bahrain Airport. Don't worry, they had said, you will be taken care of. But what about our luggage? It would be off-loaded here, along with all the camera equipment. Oh, lovely, just lovely. No visas, no permission to bring a camera into the country. This was going to be a night to remember.

"No, you cannot bring that recording camera into Bahrain. Which newspaper do you represent? I have never heard of Global Television newspaper. The camera must remain here."

"Here" was a Customs shed piled high with boxes, some worryingly empty, others with seized microwaves, TVs, radios and other electronic stuff, waiting for their rightful or wrongful owners to claim them. And it was here that we were going to leave $100,000 worth of camera gear. Oh, Toronto will be pleased! But there was some good news. A Biman rep announced that a bus would take everyone to a hotel and Biman would pick up the tab, including all meals. Reg thought he heard the word "Sheraton" amid the babble of Arabic, Urdu and Hindi. Excellent! A shower, a few beers, a steak, maybe, and a bit of a lie-down.

The bus was there all right, but it was a very small bus. A twelve-seater. Even the mathematically challenged senior field producer could figure out that two hundred Bangladeshis and three Canadians do not divide into twelve.

"Don't worry, my friend. Don't worry. There'll be another bus here in a very few minutes. My other friend has gone to get the driver."

Yeah, sure, and the Pope is Jewish.

So the twelve-seater was magically converted into a fifty-seater, or stander, or hanger-on-the-doorer. It had to be the heat; Miss Duncan was nowhere to be seen.

Through the darkened, empty streets, the bus chugged. The

streets got blacker and narrower and emptier. No glass towers, no sparkling hotels, no Sheraton. The bus finally stopped in the dingiest, narrowest, dirtiest street in the entire Middle East.

"Here we are," announced the driver. "This is your hotel."

"What is?"

"Here!"

"There's no hotel here!"

"Mister … over there. There."

Oh, shit.

A slab of weeping concrete with a door. Welcome to the Seef Hotel, Bahrain. Biman's retreat. A surly, sweaty man in a singlet grunted: "In there. That's your room."

"But there are three of us. Could we have three singles?"

"No. In there."

"In there" was a bug- and fly-infested pit with three army cots that stank of urine and you know what else.

"There's no toilet paper!" Delirium was probably setting in because there would be no need for toilet paper. No need for Lomotil or any other diarrhea drugs. If you get the shits, go straight to the Seef Hotel, Bahrain, and look in the toilet bowl. That'll stop you. Not only was there no toilet paper, there were no towels, soap, drinking water, fans or air conditioning. But there were lots of spiders and other things that crawled in the night. A couple of hours later came the dawn, and our three heroes were roused from their scratching, itching, sweating and farting by an even worse stench that came with a kind of gurgling. There, just beneath the window, in the mystic Arabian Gulf, was a sheep's head in a wheel-barrow. The best room in the majestic Seef Hotel overlooked the Bahrain abattoir.

Can I go home now, please?

No, because two days later, the Sheikh gave his plane back and we took off again for Dhaka.

To record TV images of the famine meant leaving the Dhaka Intercontinental Hotel at 4:00 AM and driving for eight hours through blistering heat and never-ending seas of humanity. The jeep slammed and pounded its way toward the Himalayan foothills, caking the camera gear and us in thick layers of dust. This trip occurred just before the video revolution. Our CP16 camera's 16-millimeter film with its audio magnetic stripe was housed on top in a "magazine" that resembled Mickey Mouse ears. Like any film, it would be ruined if light got into the magazine, so Reg checked that the film housing was screwed very tight and he kept air-gunning dust away from the lens and other mechanisms. But it was sure taking a massive pounding. And I nagged him all the way up and all the way back: "Is the camera okay, Reg? Are you sure the sides of the magazine aren't working loose? Why don't you wrap the magazine with gaffer tape and make sure it doesn't get loose?"

"Sure. John. Sure," replied a patient but weary Reg.

Death. Nothing but death. We had arrived at our destination. Some skeletons still had flesh on them, some not. It was a plain of cadavers bestridden with vultures, and swarming with flies and maggots. On the riverbank lay man and mud; from the opposite bank, low moans. The drought that had baked the crops dry turned the fields into steel, too hard to bury all the bodies, too hard to bury disease. Too hard for a country to bear.

After filming this terrible Hieronymus Bosch tableau, we bounced and choked the eight hours back to Dhaka and reached the hotel around 10:00 PM, exhausted but satisfied we had film of horror on a scale never before seen in the West; famine at its most egregious and affronting.

We unloaded the jeep, dragged the gear to the elevator and pressed "3." The doors closed slowly with a resentful whine. Just as the elevator began its ascent, we heard a clicking noise, a kind a rattling. In a nano-second of self-denial, I brushed off the noise. Probably the elevator shaft. But that was shock protecting me from the source of the real problem: where that noise was really coming from—the camera, more specifically, the magazine. Despite the tape, despite our paranoia to keep it airtight and dust free, sixteen hours in a jeep had finally exacted its toll. The side of the magazine fell open and the film spooled onto the floor of the elevator. Now exposed and utterly useless. Reg turned ashen and began trembling. Tears filled his eyes. He went to his room, hung the "Do Not Disturb" sign on his door and, I suspect, wept himself to sleep.

10

Who's a Greedy Boy?

"Arobbery will cost you $1,000 U.S. A drug raid, $5,000 and a gang raid $10,000."

The person with the price list was one of Moscow's police chiefs. The CBC had already given him the mandatory bottle of Johnnie Walker Black Label and a bottle of fine French perfume for his wife or mistress. He took the gifts perfunctorily, offered no thanks and then stated the price list for television crews who wanted to film his boys at work. This was a decade after the collapse of the Soviet Union and everything was for sale. You want to film the secret VIP underground nuclear shelter somewhere under Moscow? That will cost you $20,000. A Japanese crew just paid that. The Hermitage in St. Petersburg, $1,200. And where did all this money go? Not the government, that's for sure. The really underpaid cops would halt your car if they didn't like its color, or if you stopped one inch behind a mandatory white line, and they would ask for money. We paid a few rubles to avoid a hassle, but the police chief was too rich for our budget.

At the Hermitage itself, cameraman Louis de Guise caught the curator on camera trying to extract his dollar of flesh from the Canadians. He got nothing, nor did we.

Foreigners would pay grossly inflated prices for domestic air tickets and a boarding pass; but the plane was inevitably full and your seat was already sold to the highest bidder by the time you reached the right airport (Moscow has three). Often the flight would be cancelled without explanation for three days in a row. The only way to get the seat back was to put down a fresh, new $100 bill at the check-in, although this was often a bad idea. The Russian fleet was mechanically challenged, and passengers stood, smoked and swigged vodka as the plane took off. At one refueling stop, a local airport restaurant was closed. Why? Because it was lunchtime. How much to get it open? Twenty dollars.

And the price to fly through restricted airspace and land illegally in Murmansk, the home of the Russian nuclear fleet? One thousand dollars. That also allowed us to park our chartered plane at the highly secret submarine base for three days. It was night when we landed, and local anti-nuclear activists guided us to a small hotel with no wishing well but with the usual surly, utterly unhelpful lump behind the front desk.

"No rooms," grumped the lump without looking at her booking sheet or us.

"But your whole hotel is empty. You don't have one reservation. You do have rooms and we want six." Pushy associate producer, Corinne Seminoff, had been through this routine a hundred times during her tenure in Russia and wasn't going to lose here, even if it was a super-secret base. The woman was loaded, filled to the brim, belching a bellyful of borscht and a bucket of vodka. She may well have been used as a nuclear deterrent during the Cold War, but now she was merely a slothful slut who I hoped was leaking radiation and not the liquid it appeared to be.

"So that's six rooms," demanded Ms. Seminoff.

"No. Go away."

This charade went on for another fifteen minutes. Then, as in most hotels in the glorious Soviet system, it ended suddenly, keys handed over with no apologies, no explanations and no thank-yous. I did hear Corinne whisper, "bitch," but I'm assured that's Russian for "sweetheart." And up we went to bed. Corinne, correspondent Don Murray, cameraman Louis de Guise, soundman Tony Hill, and me. The pilots went somewhere less conspicuous. It sounded like "bath house," but I knew that couldn't be true. Who would want a bath at this time of night?

We rose at four the next morning. Three activists straight out of an old black and white movie, in long coats, and hats pulled well down, were about to take us on a very risky trip. They wanted us to tape a scene the world did not know existed. It was dangerous. If we were caught, we would most probably be arrested as spies and the activists would disappear, never to be seen again. They wanted us to tape the Russian nuclear fleet. Not the submarines at sea, but eight or so rotting in the port of Murmansk, the ones constantly leaking radiation from their still-glowing reactors. The activists had a small, motor-powered launch to ferry us out into the middle of the harbor so we could get better tracking shots and close-ups of the cancerous subs.

The dawn was grim and gray and the sea a menacing pewter. As we chugged out into the harbor, Louis began taping immediately in case we were caught. But no one appeared to have noticed us. Who would be crazy enough to land in Murmansk, hire a boat and in almost broad daylight actually tape our secret base? Naah! And I think that is exactly what happened. There were a few nervous minutes when we attempted to execute a timed piece to camera that depended on the boat turning and Don talking about the rotting subs as they wheeled into view. First take, Don blew his lines. Then Louis screwed up the focus pull. Next, the sea gave a mighty swell at the critical turning point. Finally, we got two good takes, more pictures and scuttled back to shore. All undetected.

Emboldened, the activists took us to the local hospital to see the results of those rotting underwater carcasses. On the way, we noticed gauges in the streets. There were two types. One gave the standard temperature reading, the other, that day's radiation level.

The Murmansk hospital was pitiful. But the doctors and nurses heroically allowed us into every corner of the facility, even though they, too, were taking huge risks. If they were caught letting a foreign TV crew take pictures of the suffering in Murmansk, they would be jailed. But they, too, wanted the world to know the dirty secret of Murmansk. We saw the dying and the nearly dead. And we saw a three-year-old boy. All his fingers and thumbs were bandaged in white gauze. His blonde young mother explained that the gauze was there to try to stop her son from chewing off the tops of his fingers and thumbs when the pain of his cancer became unbearable.

We flew out of Murmansk undetected. Or, I suppose, the bribe that went to the control tower was spread around and everybody was happy. Except the little boy who chewed the tops of his fingers.

The white and blue Yak 40 VIP jet we had chartered for a few black-market rubles skidded down the wet runway and whined to a halt at a hangar just outside Moscow. Next stop: the palace of the Patriarch of the Russian Orthodox Church, Alexi II. Now here was an interesting guy. Man of God and man of the KGB, the murdering secret state police with a reputation that put Hitler's Gestapo to shame. They snooped, spied, tortured, assassinated and mass-murdered the world over. For years, old Alexi insisted the initials stood for Kicks Great Butt and that he knew nothing of the organization's true activities. Sure, he traveled the world when no one else was allowed out of the old Soviet Union. And sure, even though he was a very religious man, he was a great friend of Khrushchev and all the influential members of the Communist Party. Then the rumors began to seep out. One of Alexi's fellow priests received a midnight knock on the door and was hauled off to the Gulags because he refused to sign up to assist the KGB. Killings were mentioned. Alexi denied everything, even to our cameras. But he was a liar. Secret documents found in the old KGB headquarters showed that, indeed, Alexi was a spy and possibly an assassin. He even had a code name. It was "Songthrush."

Alexi, God's singing spy. As I recall, we did not have to pay a bribe for that interview, grease anyone's palm or put a ruble in the plate. Doesn't seem right, though. Funny what tricks memories and patriarchs can get up to.

It was even funnier, but a bit more expensive in Rome. Well that's a little sacrilegious, so let us call it surprising when two popes died within a month of each other in 1978. The first to go, after thirteen years, was Pope Paul VI, or the "Peep of the People," according to reporter Rae Corelli as he flubbed his on-camera in St. Peter's Square. Paul's successor was Cardinal Albino Luciani, Pope John Paul I, who had a heart attack less than a month after his election, as did the international TV crews who had only just packed up and gone home. The European crews got back first, we a day later, by which time all the camera positions had been allocated by the Vatican Press bureau. No room for any more and no, you will not be allowed in St. Peter's Square and no, you will not be allowed inside the Basilica. You should go back to Canada. Even a very lapsed Catholic like me was tempted to pray. Hypocrisy makes strange dead fellows.

Our driver was a good Catholic, or so he told us. He turned out to be a brilliant Catholic with an understanding of the Vatican and its dark spiritual and temporal ways.

"You want a camera position, yes?"

"Yes."

"Okay, Mr. John, you come with me," into an office deep inside the world's smallest country.

He approached a priest whom he seemed to know and disappeared into an office.

"Here you are, Mr. John. Just fill out these forms." They were applications for camera positions.

"Will two positions be enough, Mr. John?"

"Yes, sure, but …"

"Mr. John," he whispered. "The father says everything is taken care of. Just give him fifty dollars on your way out."

TV crews carry large amounts of cash for those obvious reasons, usually U.S. dollars. Some foreign television stations will insist on cash in advance before accepting a satellite feed, which can run into thousands of dollars, and it is seldom known exactly where the money goes once it leaves our hands. Anywhere in the world, sane folks, especially journalists, try not to advertise the fact that they are carrying large sums of money—especially if they have a huge wad of greenbacks far in excess of the country's declarable currency allowance. Not only is there a chance of being caught by currency officers, there's always the fear that someone else has heard how much you are carrying and will follow you out the door and down the street, with only one thing in mind: your money.

At Nicosia Airport, Cyprus, which was a staging point in getting to Beirut during the civil war (taxis $300 an hour), Cypriot officials demanded currency declarations from journalists in the arrivals queue, among whom one day was a fellow Canadian TV journalist.

"How much money do you have?"

"(Mumble) thousand dollars," came the nervously whispered reply.

"How much?"

"(Mumble) thousand dollars."

"What are you saying? I can't hear you!"

Panic spread across my colleague's face. Why won't this stupid bastard shut up?

"How much?"

"Sixty thousand U.S. dollars."

"Sixty thousand U.S. dollars!" shrieked the Cypriot, whose voice reverberated across the island, heard by every one of its three-quarters of a million inhabitants, who instantly jumped into jeeps, leaped onto buses, mounted oxen (no, no, not like that) and headed straight for the airport.

"Sixty thousand U.S. dollars! Why do you have so much money?"

Every gaze rested on the profusely sweating journalist and his wad of cash.

"I'm bringing money for my colleagues in Beirut."

"Beirut? Why didn't you say so? You may go."

But the Canadian didn't feel safe again until he was dodging bullets and bombs in downtown Beirut. Safe in Beirut … funny old world.

⇥ ● ⇤

I went to Lebanon thirteen times during the fifteen-year civil war that cost a hundred thousand lives and displaced a million people. Although it officially ended in 1990, assassinations and car bombings continue to rock the city into the twenty-first century, as Israel and the U.S. try to crush any surrogate who is not with them, especially those with nuclear potential.

During the civil war, Beirut's airport was closed for months on end, so the most assured way of getting to Lebanon was by sea. Ferries and hydrofoils plied pretty regularly between Larnaca, Cyprus and Beirut. The hydrofoil did the 125-mile crossing in about six hours but it was not pleasant. It bounced and slammed and drenched its way across the Mediterranean to the accompaniment of much retching and heaving. Still, it was a way in and, more important, a way out.

On the other hand, the car ferries took all night. They could carry several hundred passengers; they had cabins, food and drink, and were fairly stable. But even the ferries were cancelled when the fighting made docking in Beirut impossible. The passengers were usually a mixture of Lebanese businessmen, Christian families (the ones with money), journalists and other undesirables. On one memorable trip, passengers awoke to see the Beirut coastline about a mile off the starboard side, the port side, and then back to starboard—but never front on. The ferry was doing wheelies waiting for a gun battle near the docks to subside. When one artillery round slammed into the water very close to the ship, the captain pulled further away from the shore and continued chugging around in circles.

The weather was ugly with heavy rain, high winds and a worsening sea, but not bad enough to prevent the crew from laying the tables for breakfast. The room could seat roughly a hundred diners. The ship leaned gracefully into a swell and, just as gracefully, every piece of crockery and cutlery crashed to the floor amid much cheering, whistling and applause. The crew were not amused. Determined lads, they re-laid the tables as the sea calmed a little. Out came the food, ladled onto plates: bacon, toast, eggs, hummus, pita bread, olives, cheese, soup, Arabic and Western coffee and tea, cups filled to the brim.

Then … Whoah! Another huge swell and, just as gracefully as the first time, every piece of breakfast-laden crockery and cut-lery slid in unison, off the white tablecloths and crashed to the deck. This was followed by even louder cheering and more applause. A thoroughly pissed-off waiter accosted the CBC: "Stop laughing! Stop laughing! This is not funny." But that just made it sillier.

One deck up, on the bridge, unknown to the passengers, another more serious drama was being enacted and no one was laughing. Half a dozen Lebanese businessmen were getting the idea that the captain had no intention of sailing into Beirut port this blustery, artillery-laced day. He'd make a few more circles and then headed back to Cyprus. They also understood that if he tried to dock in Beirut the crew would mutiny. No one will confirm that the businessmen held more than a metaphoric gun to the captain's head, but their threats of physical and commercial violence made him far more amenable to their demand that he sail into the port of Jounieh in Christian East Beirut. And the crew? They could take cover; only one volunteer would be needed to open one entrance. The ship would not tie up. It would come alongside, free-floating for exactly five minutes, and then put to sea again.

The general announcement was in Arabic followed by a babble of panic in Arabic and English. We had fourteen large cases of camera gear and audio equipment, four personal bags, plus hand luggage and the video camera. Nobody knew which exit would be used. The ferry turned and headed toward Jounieh as the storm became fiercer, with sheets of rain and howling winds. Even so, the weather couldn't drown out the sounds of a gun battle being fought with artillery and rocket-propelled grenades. It sounded very close.

A member of the ferry crew gripped a panel on the empty car deck. The few who wanted to risk getting off—those businessmen, a few young guys, and the CBC—held on to a railing beside him. As the ferry thudded against the dock, the now-screaming crewman heaved a side panel open.

"Yalla! Yalla!" he yelled. The boat crunched against the dock again, then lurched back about four feet. Beneath us, just open sea. The wind was howling and the rain was still pouring down, along with artillery shells.

"Yalla! Yalla!" As the ferry pitched back toward the dock, we jumped. And made it. Then the ferryman wildly hurled luggage from the boat, some of which crashed onto the dock, while the rest smacked into the water and sank.

Breathless, panting and shaken, we tried to take stock. All four of us were okay. "What about the gear? One, two, three … fourteen! It's all here! Amazing! Now what about personal bags? One, two, three. Huh? One, two, three … one didn't make it."

Whose bag was now at the bottom of Jounieh harbor? Guess.

Few of us in this business received any kind of danger pay; but in Beirut, the Commodore Hotel took good care of its guests, the foreign press, its only customers for ten years. Several other hotels took the overflow and also tried to woo the press trade, but the Commodore had potent weapons, one of its most effective being its billing system. The Commodore opened in 1958, but it was the civil war that made it. Says the hotel's own promotional material of the war years: *"Around its sturdy bar sat a steady stream of journalists, politicians, spies and UN Peacekeepers."* Spies? Well, John le Carré based himself at the Commodore while researching his latest novel. But they left out BBC radio reporter Chris Drake's parrot that gave deafening, uncannily accurate impressions of bombs falling. The publicity blurb goes on: *"Famous for its quality of service and its ability to cater to every wish …"*

Did it ever.

The hotel staff, under the lovely and shrewd manager, Mr. Fouad, and his companion, Rita, would see us coming back at the end of another day covering the war. The bar was always ready with the coldest beers in the Middle East, and if you cared to enquire, it was not too hard to find other synapse-snapping aids such as heroin and cocaine, although the suppliers of these tended to be found among the press corps. Also on tap: Algerian or Zimbabwean passports, fifty bucks each; driving licenses from your country of choice, twenty bucks; gold? How much do you want? The wild, wild West Beirut. And knowing that some of us were being killed, wounded or turning psychotic without proper compensation, the Commodore made things disappear: meal charges seldom found their way onto your bill, and bar charges evaporated. When you ordered a beer, Youseff, the barman, would always solemnly ask: "Room number, please?" And a chorus of numbers would erupt: 205, 166, 103. It was all part of the evening's entertainment, which was halted one night by two Shia gunmen who stormed into the hotel and emptied their AK47s into the finest booze in the bar, along with the worst. But this being Beirut, the bar was back in business the next night, and the Shia were told not to do that again, please, or Fouad would stop paying them their protection money.

I did not witness this next incident—one of the reliable tales from the Commodore book of common lore, emerging from one of the fiercest bombardments of the war. It went on for days while all the guests huddled in the basement. Above ground, the hotel changed from guesthouse to ghost house. Nothing moved. On the second night, one thirsting scribe could stand it no longer. In pitch darkness, he crawled on his belly out of the basement and up the stairs. He could hear gunfire but it seemed to be coming from outside the hotel, not inside. He snaked along the floor until he reached the bar. With a nose that twitched when it came within three feet of single malt Scotch, he gingerly wrapped his fingers around what he knew to be a bottle of his heavenly elixir, lifted it gently from the shelf, tucked it under his sweater, and was about to slither back to the basement, when Youseff popped his head over the bar.

"Room number, please?"

So what happened to those bar bills? Suffice it to say that neither the guests nor the hotel paid for the self-awarded danger money. Let's just say it was creative accounting, Commodore-style.

Back to the blurb:

> The Beirut Commodore's luck ran out in 1987, when it was caught in the cross-fire of fighting between rival militias and had to close its doors. The Hotel was officially re-opened on February 1996, in the presence of Ministers, Ambassadors, businessmen and dignitaries. After an ambitious three-year, 50 million dollar construction project, the Beirut Commodore has emerged as the first international five-star hotel in the Beirut area. What the press remembers is not what they're going to see.

Pity.

The Green Line in Beirut had nothing to do with conservation and was surely not about saving the planet. It was an artificial divide between the Christian east and the Muslim west, policed for two years by four armies of the UN multinational force, Italy, France, the U.S. and the U.K., sucked into the maelstrom by a fretful but not totally committed international community. That would have meant condemning Israel, which just wasn't, and isn't done. So, in went four powerful nations to sort out these bloody Arabs, Palestinians or whatever. The UN forces blocked all access routes across the city except one, a main avenue that was opened at dawn and closed at dusk, or when the fighting became too intense.

The Green Line was the title of one of our CBC documentaries. Most days at dawn, around 6:00 AM, a UN soldier would swing back the heavy iron gates blocking the road, and Beirut would be open for business. We left the Commodore Hotel at five and drove the twenty minutes to the Green Line. Sunni Muslim fighters, known as the Mourabitoun, were already crouched behind a wall of sandbags awaiting starter's orders. They were armed with assault rifles, rocket launchers and mortars that would give the city another almighty wake-up call.

As night slowly surrendered to day, a French UN soldier dragged open the clanking, scraping gate. Two cars from the Christian East crawled across the imaginary line into West Beirut. Trucks on the Muslim side laden with fruit inched forward. Three men in suits, money dealers or launderers, tiptoed into their other world. Another day had dawned in the city that would not die.

Then, *boom*, and the place erupted into hysteria—mortars, grenades, rifles and machine guns—heavy fighting after a good night's rest. About fifty meters behind the Mourabitoun, two men emerged from a four-storey apartment block that was taking heavy hits from Christian rockets. They were not evacuating the building, which would have made sense. They were carrying a coffin. They calmly loaded it onto the roof of their car, tied it down and drove off. They were probably afraid of waking the dead. Cameraman Michael Sweeney, as always, got the shot, and we huddled down behind the sandbags looking for a chance to either get more pictures or get the hell out of there. At this moment, soundman Alister Bell chose to remind me of last night's phone call home to Toronto, one of the few I'd been able to make.

"So, John, how does it feel? Here you are being shot at in a shithole at six in the morning, while your wife's off ballroom dancing in New York and your son's told you he wants to become a priest!" At least Al's merry quips broke the tension ... so I broke his nose. Just kidding.

Later that morning, we drove through the Chouf mountains to meet a group of Druze (a branch of Islam) militiamen who were eager to show us something very rare—the bodies of two pilots from the Lebanese air force, which had a total of two planes that belonged to the Christians. They had taken off from a secret strip everyone knew about north of Jounieh, and the Druze gunners shot them down over the Chouf. The airmen lay on a hillside, rotting in their uniforms and flight gear. Dignity in death? They were shown none. On the way back, we were stopped at one of the many checkpoints set up by anyone with a gun. Usually they wanted money (one Palestinian even gave me a receipt); but this particular guy in a Muslim uniform wanted our prized flak jackets. We knew this because he pointed his AK47 first at our heads and then at the jackets. Ahbed, our driver from the Commodore, had had enough. We'd endured a very long, sickening day. Exhausted and quite cranky, Ahbed let fly with a stream of abuse so intense, the bewildered hijacker forgot he had a gun, apologized and waved us through.

Ahbed knew Lebanon and he knew where the stories were. One morning he took us to a Christian cemetery on the edge of the Green Zone. An old man, weeping tears of despair that soaked his week-old stubble, urged the people with the camera to come with him, to see what "those animals" had done. The animals, more or less of the human kind, were allegedly Shia gunmen, but whoever they were, they had mighty strong stomachs. Perhaps as many as thirty skeletons were strewn about the graveyard, many still in their best burial clothes that had not decayed at the same rate as their flesh. All dressed up and nowhere to go. The dead had been ripped from the aboveground mausoleums and attacked with hatchets. Rib cages crushed, skulls disintegrated. At least they were dead. Only the living felt the pain at the desecration wreaked by the madmen.

Not that the Christians were mere victims. In the suburb of Ein Romanei, our car turned a corner to reveal a line of a dozen Muslim prisoners being marched single file to a military base. When they saw our camera, the Christian Phalange escorts screamed at us to put the camera down or they would shoot. No wonder. Under a bridge nearby we saw what they had done to five other Muslim prisoners. They were splayed, stiff and stinking; one's guts were hanging out, another's stomach lining billowed in the breeze like a grounded weather balloon.

•

For the living, death was a way of life, and the wise one shunned the healers who repaired damaged bodies before inevitable death befell them in tormented, bloody Beirut.

"Get out of the car!"

The hospital was a good—no, make that, bad—fifty meters from the guarded entrance.

"I can't," I pleaded, "I've hurt my ankle"—while diving for cover in the mountain town of Abbeh. The dive, a forward somersault with tuck, was executed as shells slammed into the street. They had been launched from the USS *New Jersey*, a Second World War battleship prowling off the coast of Lebanon.

"You walk."

Thanking him ("asshole" is a term of endearment in Arabic), it took me only ten minutes of hopping, stepping, but not much jumping, to reach the entrance.

"Please wait here. Now you must pay before the doctor will see you. One hundred Lebanese pounds" (about five bucks).

"Fine. Here you are."

"No. You must take it to the cashier."

"Where's the cashier?"

"Down that corridor and to the right."

"But I've got a bad ankle. In fact, both ankles are injured. I can't walk. Can't you take the money?"

In a stunning act, completely out of character for a Lebanese, he refused to take the money.

"No. You must pay and come back with a receipt. Then the doctor will see you."

Money paid, on the hop, the doctor arrived.

"Hello, mister. How did you hurt your arm?"

"No, doctor, it's both my ankles."

"Okay. First, we'll get them X-rayed."

"Where do we do that?"

"In the next cubicle. But first you have to pay, then we X-ray."

"How much?"

"One hundred Lebanese pounds."

No, he would not take it, but he did require a cashier's receipt. But my ankles? Did he have a wheelchair?

Hop, shuffle, hop.

"Here are the X-rays Mr. Surry. Both your ankles are broken. Now, I can put them in plaster or I can bandage them."

Both legs in plaster, applied in a hospital in Beirut? Uh, I think not.

"Okay, I'll bandage them. But first …"

Hop, shuffle, hop.

The experts at the Commodore thought I should get a second opinion—at the U.S. Marine base—but the doc was out on an urgent call; the wind had come up and the surfing was great.

"I'm the medical officer on duty. What's wrong?"

"The hospital says both my ankles are broken, but I'd really appreciate it if you could take a look."

"Sure, no problem, sir. Now, which elbow is it?"

It couldn't get any better than this, could it?

"Well, I've got to admit, Mr. Sutty, sir, I've never done an X-ray before, but I guess we all gotta start somewhere."

At which he opened a manual: *How to X-ray*.

"Hmm. This should be a cinch. Now, what knee was it again?"

⇥ ● ⇤

War zones attract the very best and the very worst in our profession. Novices are in the greatest danger, often trying to make a name for themselves or get established as freelancers. One Canadian kid was desperate to get a job on a national newspaper as a photographer but couldn't break through the wall. So he decided to risk everything and go to Sarajevo, taking pictures he hoped no Canadian paper could refuse. On his very first day, a sniper shot him in the back and he died instantly. He was in the wrong place at the wrong time and was not wearing a flak jacket.

Then there are the "cowboys" in war zones—those who take too many risks, believing themselves unkillable. A few carry guns, although most don't, still believing that journalists are neutral non-combatants. However, embedding and hired security out-riders made it tougher to be neutral, especially when your guard opens fire on a perceived threat.

We had a cowboy on one of our CBC crews in Lebanon, although none of us guessed it until an incident in the hills high above Beirut. The day's objective was to reach a town in which thousands of Christians had been cut off for a month from the rest of civilization (the word is used loosely) by a Druze blockade. Conditions in the town were said to be desperate—illness, star-vation and death. The officer in charge of the Druze roadblock was fiftyish, wore a neat gray beard and was polite but little more. I could imagine him as a history teacher. He wanted to see the CBC's letter of accreditation from the Druze high command. We had one, written in Arabic.

One of the perils of covering a war with so many different factions is the pass system. You have to have official passes from every militia if you want to get around. And you have to carry all of them with you all of the time. In this particular situation, we had passes from the Christians, the Palestinians, the Druze, Sunni Muslims, Shia Muslims, Amal, the Mourabitoun; you had to be careful to show the right one. A Shia gunman would not be amused if you showed him your Christian pass. All of them were in Arabic, so I put tiny, barely perceptible marks on mine: "c" for Christian on the top left of the pass, "s" for Shia, and so on.

The Druze officer wanted to search the car to make sure there was no food, drink or weapons being smuggled in to the trapped Christians. Our gear included lights, a tripod, microphones, battery belts that looked like bandoleers, cables and flak jackets—five cases in all. One of the rules at roadblocks, or in life for that matter, is never show them anything they don't ask to see. But this officer wanted to see it all.

"Open this."

As he peered inside one particular silver case, his eyes widened. At the bottom lay half a dozen shell casings. Our own CBC cowboy was a collector of guns, ammunition and all things military. Whacko aficionado, I believe, is the Latin term for him. It took some talking, but eventually the Druze guy accepted whatever lie we made up. But then, before we could stop him, the insouciantly stupid, self-ingratiating cowboy reached inside the car and hauled out the flak jackets.

"Have you seen how these things work? On the inside panel here, there's this zip. You undo it like this, and here's the material that stops the bullets."

Written in very large letters in English and Hebrew: "Made in Israel."

Jeezus Christ!! He'll think we're Israeli military, maybe spies! Oh, fuck!

But although he spoke good English, it appeared the officer could not read or recognize either written language.

The CBC did not get to the trapped Christian village that day.

The Druze officer ordered us out of the area. It was all too suspicious for his liking.

We dumped the jackets and the cowboy.

11

Sir, Please Tighten
Your Sphincter

alking of dumping, of the bodily kind, the World Health Organization estimates a million and a half people, mainly kids under five, die from the entirely preventable disease diarrhea. I have already mentioned one simple solution: clean drinking water makes a dramatic difference. So why isn't tanker load after tanker load being shipped or flown around the clock to those who are dying? The terrible answer is that our governments would rather fly guns and gasoline around the clock because that's where the money is, and fighting diarrhea doesn't give you much mileage in the War on Terror. We privileged journalists take pills and precautions, but they do not always work.

Whenever you get sick in a shithole, the correct procedure is to check in immediately, not to the local hospital but to the airport departure lounge. No good will come of it if you stay. The most common deficiencies are lack of water, lack of hygiene, lack of drugs, a lack of knowledge and some rather curious customs.

It has many names: the squits, the shits, Delhi belly, Montezuma's revenge, gastro, diarrhea. Whatever you call it, it's a big pain in the—you-know-where. One of my colleagues was suddenly hit by it on a street in Jerusalem. Almost without warning he exploded. Rivers of it. His trousers were instantly transformed into stained, wet and stinking brown hip waders. He tried to clean himself up in a nearby toilet and then, half standing, half sitting, was driven back to his hotel as the driver tried not to laugh and gag at the same time. Hoping that no one in the lobby would notice him—the grimaces, the gasps and hurried handkerchiefs pulled over noses and mouths indicated no one had missed this sight, although it was not on that day's tourist agenda—he took the attended elevator to his floor and waddled to his room. There he showered, changed his clothes, and for the next two days wore a towel as a diaper in case it happened again. The shits can be much more serious, but seldom more embarrassing.

Most of us journalists have trained ourselves in the unhealthy practice of going without a bowel evacuation for days at a time. Combined with jet lag, fatigue and insufficient non-alcoholic fluids, you have the perfect recipe for ... impacted stools! Thank you, Jesus. Impacted stools are medically dangerous and need to be removed quickly before they do internal damage. You feel as if someone has rammed a brick up your rectum and cemented it in. That means you cannot walk, you lose your appetite, lose your penchant for high jumping and, of course, you cannot do that which you most crave. Acknowledged treatments include dynamite and rocket-propelled grenades; surgery is an alternative—or a visit to the hospital in the former Soviet Union republic of Tajikistan, the capital of which is Dushanbe, pronounced douche-on-bay.

I realized I had an immovable brickload when I tried to go to the washroom in my hotel room. A sympathetic, unsmirking associate producer, Corinne Seminoff, offered me help from her precious supply of purgatives, but to no avail. The city was under curfew that night and its gas fuel supply had run dry, so it seemed I would remain stuck, as it were. But in the hotel, the local Red Crescent heard of my plight from one of the crew and did an extraordinarily courageous thing. They siphoned a car of what gas it had left, poured it into their ambulance, and then, in pitch black, lights off, broke the curfew and crawled to the local hospital. Here, the doctors are professional, generous and kind, but they are not well trained in the gentle art of stool removal; however, they *are* enthusiastic.

The doctor instructed the poor correspondent, Don Murray, to stay in the room and translate. Don has had hundreds of horrific assignments in his career, but few could match this one.

"He wants you to tighten your sphincter, John." Wow, Don knew the Russian word for sphincter. The doctor was a jolly man who relished the challenge.

"He wants you to lie on your side and bring your knees up to your chest. Good. Now he's going to have a look up"—with a periscope that might have come from an old Russian submarine.

"Aaahh!"

"Uh-haa!"

Oh, God, he's unreeling a hose.

Up it went. Aaahh!

"Yes, yes, very good, mister."

Not really.

He pulled out the hose, phhht! But nothing came with it. However, this man would not be beaten. Up it went again with even more water pressure.

"Aaah! Oooh!"

Phht!

"Yaa!" shrieked the doctor as a turd rocketed across the room. "We try some more."

An hour and a dozen flying turds later, the battle of the bum was over. The doctor refused to take one ruble. It had been his pleasure.

→═ ● ═←

And now let me whisk you away to the tropical island of Grenada in the Caribbean, with a mainly English-speaking population of one hundred thousand. In 1974 it was about to declare independence from Britain and a struggle for power had begun. Civil war was imminent. There'd been mass arrests, some shooting, but no casualties yet. It was tense in this Garden of Eden, and the foreign press poured in: the big U.S. networks, the Brits, the Germans and the Canadians.

The first story we did for Global News in Toronto was a scene-setter: the situation and an explanation of the main players and the volatility of the whole island. Telephone links with the outside world were down. Our film reports were flown out, until they closed the airport for "security reasons." To communicate with Toronto, Brian Kelly, Dan Laffey, Tony Hillman and I had to go to the local Cable and Wireless office to send and receive telex messages. The first one from Toronto was a "herogram"—"great work, blah, blah, blah."

I was reading this to Tony Hillman as we walked out of Cable and Wireless, but my distracted exit was not by the door. I walked straight through a plate-glass window. I thought the top of my head had been sliced off. Blood spurted from my right hand and left leg. The glass had slashed an artery. In a moment of further buffoonery, I turned around, leaking badly, and went back to the counter to apologize to the gentlemen at Cable and Wireless for breaking their window. They gaped with incredulity.

"Go to hospital! Go to hospital!"

That was good advice, but then, not so good. With the island cut off, Grenada's hospital had run out of most everything: needles, sutures, painkillers and bandages. There were blood-covered swabs on the floor amid flies and dirt.

"Oh, you shouldn't have come here."

These words of comfort and reassurance came from the doctor.

"You should have gone to Barbados."

With an artery pumping merrily away and a closed airport?

"Well, I'm sorry but we have only a tiny amount of anesthetic left."

He asked the nurse for a needle to inject the morphine. She dropped it on the floor, picked it up and jabbed it in.

"We don't have any proper stitches left so these will have to do."

The sutures were probably once a tennis racket.

Then: "I'm sorry we don't have any new bandages but these ones have been washed."

And finally: "I'm sorry but you should have gone to Barbados."

As it turned out, I was the only casualty of the war that never was.

Back in Toronto, the staff at the Wellesley Hospital were in stitches. Mine.

"Hey, come and look at this! Over here! You gotta see this!"

When they stopped laughing enough, they removed the tennis

strings. Over thirty years later my right thumb still hurts like hell, it's still swollen and it's still a bit deformed.

Yeah, I know. I should have gone to Barbados.

⇥ ● ⇤

One of India's major Hindu holidays is "holidays" without the "days": Holi. It's a rite of spring, a time of great joy and merriment. Like festivities in most places, the men get drunk, the women get annoyed and merrymakers pour paint-to-dye-for all over each other: families, friends, perfect strangers, imperfect ones, too. Holi, the Festival of Color.

Let me take you to the Holy Holi city of Varanasi, or Benares, one of the oldest cities in the world. It is also perhaps the most popular cremation center in India, popular with everyone except the crematee.

The mighty holy Ganges River flows through Varanasi. Along with it flow cows, prairie dogs, lions, tigers, armadillos, monkeys, hippopotami, razor-backed pigs and elephants. And, of course, sewage.

A pilgrimage to Varanasi is de rigueur for the Hindu faithful who bathe in the holy Ganges and drink in its waters. Then they die. The dead are dipped in one last time then laid on a bed of sticks, covered with more sticks and finally slathered with ghee— or clarified butter, which goes great with lobsters and corpses. A monk does a few sprints around the pyre, sprinkles odor-reducing powders, and then up she, or he, goes!

Some really wholly holy, Holi men called sadhus (when in India do as the sadhus) live on the cremation grounds. Their diet is strictly non-vegetarian. It's not so much what they eat, but whom. You want fries with that corpse? After a full-bodied meal, the sadhus cover themselves with ashes, anyone's, and meditate the day away. They're off limits to the holier than thou. No paint for them, but for everyone else this day, it's splash and trash.

After filming some of these eye-catching, nose-twitching scenes, it was back to the hotel, miraculously undyed and undead. Except for our soundman, Keith Bonnell. He was squirting rose-colored diarrhea. No one had painted his Newfie bum pink that we had seen, so what malodorous, mystic, multicolored malady had befallen him? We called for a doctor.

There was Keith, squirting and vomiting splendid rainbows and well on his way to becoming a sadhu's afternoon snack, when we heard a tap-tap-tap on the door. In staggered a small man, painted black from head to toe and wearing just a loincloth. Keith thought he had died and gone to hell, not that he wasn't already there. The black-painted vision adjusted his little loincloth, bobbled slightly and announced in booze-slurred English: "I'm the doctor. What sheems to be the trouble?"

Amoebic dysentery.

A Holi terror.

Note: Keith spent a week in the hospital, and we got him a private room with a TV. He got better but complained it was the most boring week of his life. All he did was watch TV in Hindi. Silly boy didn't think to change the channel. CNN and BBC were one click away.

12

Men of War

Keith should have been grateful he did not have a laptop with him. Then he could have been really sick. If you type a couple of keywords into any search engine you can watch videos so grotesque you wonder why anyone would or could sit through them without throwing up. I'm talking assassinations, murders and common, old, garden-variety beheadings. Except that the beheadings are not as neat and brisk as one would imagine. They are endurance tests of horror, as amateur butchers slice, chop, stab and hack away at the victim's neck until the head finally comes away, gushing streams of blood onto the killer and flooding the floor. It's not a pretty sight, or site, but it is effective.

Terror is effective. But we can take it because it doesn't happen to us, right? Wrong. Terror has been used to suppress the truth that journalists uncover, and it is being used more and more. They beheaded Wall Street journalist Daniel Pearl for trying to find out a truth about Iraq. If you have had the grotesque misfortune to see a beheading on the internet, you might agree with me that it is the most powerful argument for censorship ever seen. Anyone with a computer, at any age, or in any state of mind, can simply hit "enter" and see a stream of recorded beheadings. Their hooded perpetrators cannot be men of God, but men of ultimate evil.

They may praise Allah, but they are delusional. They are terrorists. The screaming, whimpering, gasping victims die the most traumatic, shocking death no human should ever have to endure, or see. Internet carriers should pull these obscenities off the Net the moment they appear. Just as they would pictures of men raping babies. I had never advocated censorship of any kind until I saw the beheadings. They may be weapons of terror, but they are moments of human degradation with which only live pictures of child pornography can compare.

The murder of journalists is used as a weapon of terror around the world. Over a hundred have been executed in Central America for revealing the activities of the killers (government and guerrilla) in the drug cartels in Colombia and the activities of the Latino gangs in El Salvador. Of course, they don't only kill journalists. A favorite ploy of a Latino gang is to kill an innocent female to instil terror into her family or her gang-member brother. In the Vietnam War, sixty-six journalists were killed in ten years. In Iraq, that many died in three years alone. In World War II, the number of journalists killed was sixty-nine. Sixty-nine. In Iraq, the number surpassed two hundred in 2007. But all these are mere numbers. Let me put some faces and reasons to them, including my own.

Journalists are killed for many reasons. In war zones, they can be literally dead-unlucky, just plain stupid or real targets. But most of all, journalists are killed because they try to disprove lies, prove and show truths, and make the powerful uncomfortable, so they must be controlled, even if that means death.

Nothing is going to protect you from a five-hundred-kilogram bomb, an artillery shell lobbed fifty kilometers away or a badly aimed rocket-propelled grenade. News camera crews get killed simply because they always have to be where the action is. But a stunning number of radio reporters are also killed (over sixty in the past ten years), not always in battle but often simply because they refused to broadcast a manifesto by the local guerrilla leader, or because they criticized one of the thug governments in Colombia, the former Soviet Union, and parts of Asia and Africa. That kind of reporting, along with cyber-journalists and newspaper men and women in dictatorships such as China, Ethiopia and Zimbabwe, requires unimaginable courage and conviction and nearly always means harassment, jail, torture or death. Helmets and flak jackets are of no use to them.

Here are some of my rules for covering wars. Some are arbitrary, some just gut instinct, others rules to live or die by. I repeat, these are my own personal rules. If you choose to follow them, don't blame me if they don't work and you get killed.

- Don't leave home unless your organization has enough money to equip you properly: bullet-proof jackets, helmets and, if possible, armored vehicles, communication equipment, survival and first-aid gear; make sure they will pay those massive insurance bills and are willing to spend even more to get you out in a hurry. I worked for a company who assured me I had war insurance, e.g., $20,000 if I lost a leg, $30,000 for an eye and $250,000 if I got killed. Trouble was, they lied. One night, in an alcoholic stupor, the company treasurer confessed they had been running short of cash and the war insurance would have put them in the red. So they had taken a chance and sent me and a crew off to war without a penny's coverage. I left the company a few days later.

- Before you leave home, tell your family to sue your company if you get killed or maimed. That way, they are covered if—and I can't believe this would ever happen (yeah, right)—the insurance company was tardy or argumentative. A colleague of mine was killed in Lebanon while working as a freelance reporter for a North American network. They offered his widow three months' pay. She sued and got a lot, lot more. Now Reporters Without Borders is arranging cheap rates for freelancers with an ultimate payout of nearly $2 million.

- Hire a driver who is fearless but smart enough to know when to be frightened.

- Control your own fear by focusing on being a journalist, but know that fear is good if it keeps you alive.

- On any particular day, if you assess your chances of being killed at 50 percent, those are good odds, so you go about your job. Reason? By merely arriving in a war zone, your chances of being killed have doubled. If you don't fancy those odds, go home. If the percentage goes above 65, it's time to adopt defensive tactics. How do I get my percentages? They comprise a combination of how free you are to move about the area; where the front lines are; how much of the stuff is incoming; are there snipers; are the guys at the roadblocks drunk or on drugs; are you dealing with a professional army or a militia; have any of your colleagues been killed, injured or had calls that were too close; and can you get good pictures and sound and tell a meaningful story without getting yourself or a member of your team injured or killed?

- If the danger is 65 percent or higher, decide in the morning before you leave your hotel (if it's still standing), what exactly you can film in two hours, then get the hell back. Repeat the procedure in the afternoon. Don't try anything at night unless it's shots from a well-protected balcony. In the hotel, you may have options, such as filling your tub with water if there's a chance the building could be hit and catch fire. It is also a source of drinking (after being heavily dosed with purifying tablets or fed through portable filters) and washing water if the pipes get blown to pieces. But the tub can provide another protection … as a bed. If you are in the heart of a conflict zone, bombs and other weapons can shatter windows miles away, so always put lashings of tape across your windows to try to prevent them from shattering. A hit or near-miss might blow the glass, the entire frame and other parts of the room unhappily in your direction. But if you put your mattress in the tub, lie very low and, yes, close the door, you might have a chance of surviving. If the attack is sudden and you are not prepared, either dive under the bed, or, if possible, run like hell to the basement, if there is one. If not, bye, bye. And look after your team. Are they safe? Do they have food, heat and water? Just how scared are they? I remember having to send one audio person home because fear had paralyzed him, leaving him unable to work, unable to take precautions to keep himself alive.
- If you are traveling in a convoy, either with military or

just media, never be the first or the last vehicle. They are the most vulnerable positions in an ambush. And if there are just two cars? Do you believe in prayer?

- Never carry weapons. We are unbiased observers, not combatants, although this area has become very muddy as crews travel with armed "security advisors" and insurance companies' demands get more stringent and exorbitant.

- Never go into a war zone to make a name for yourself. Go in for the story, otherwise you're likely to take really stupid risks and die.

- Resist telling war stories. Everyone else finds them and you a boring pain in the ass.

So, let me tell you another war story,

The crew did all the right things but, even so, it all went wrong. Bill Stewart was a reporter for the American ABC television network. I had run into him just once during yet another major Israeli attack on Hezbollah militias in south Lebanon. He seemed a bit of a loudmouth, a cocky U.S. hotshot. The next time I saw Bill Stewart, he was on television, reporting from Nicaragua. The ABC crew had stopped about fifty meters from a roadblock manned by soldiers still loyal to the about-to-be-defeated dictator, Anastasio Somoza. The camera was secretly recording from the back seat as Stewart stepped out of their van, followed by translator Juan Espinosa, and walked, hands in the air, toward the soldiers. It was the right move. Roadblocks, if you'll forgive the expression, are minefields. The last thing you do is leap out of the vehicle with the camera rolling. That really pisses a lot of soldiers right off. So you approach them with a big smile on your face;

you offer to shake their hands, which sometimes confuses them, makes them less decisive; and they often feel the need to return your friendliness, smile back and wave you on.

There was a pause when Stewart and Espinosa reached the roadblock. As a viewer at home, I could hear no sounds apart from the breathing of the cameraman, Jack Clark, in the van. There seemed to be a short conversation between Stewart and one of the soldiers. Stewart dropped to his knees, hands behind his head. Then he lay facedown on the road. The cameraman's breathing got heavier: "Oh, Jesus, they're going to kill him." The soldier took one step forward, kicked Stewart in the side, and shot him in the back of the head. His body flipped into the air and flopped back as the bullet tore his life away. Then they killed Espinosa. Losers hate the press.

Stewart's death was televised around the world and a shocked U.S. government raged: "They can't do that to one of our boys!" They suddenly withdrew their support for their buddy, their Commie-fighting hero Somoza, who was ousted by the Sandinista guerrilla army one month later.

David Blundy was a tall, gangly, great British journalist who was often not completely sober. The last time we met was in Tripoli, Libya, when Ron the Film Star Cowboy decided to bomb Colonel Gaddafi back to the stone age for some reprehensible act like the Lockerbie bombing of Pan Am 103, killing 270 people, or providing weapons to the IRA, or giving nuclear technology to both India and Pakistan, or for wearing silly hats. Whatever, Ronnie wanted to bomb Gaddafi. Problem was, his planes missed and killed a few of the Colonel's kids.

At the time, there was no drier country in the world than

Libya … it didn't rain much, either. Only Iran could match Libya's green-flagged zealotry to ban the greatest evil any axis has known: booze. Get caught and it's goodbye mum, goodbye dad, hello nice Mr. Jailer. Can I have my beating now, please? Thank you so much.

So I was surprised when the phone rang in our edit suite in the Al Kabir hotel.

"Scully! Come down to my room right now. It's an emergency."

Blundy was tired as a newt, right under the Colonel's nose, and he wanted to share a little—but not too much—of his good fortune. As a relentless, probing newspaper man, he went to the British Embassy for an "off-the-record briefing." I believe the diplomat who briefed him went down in Blundy's notes as Mr. Johnnie Walker.

The next time I saw David Blundy, like Bill Stewart, he was on a TV screen. One of a bank of monitors in the CBC newsroom in Toronto. It was just a head-and-shoulders photograph. The wire service reports said he had been with a small group of news people who were covering a gun battle in rural El Salvador. The government said David Blundy had been caught in the crossfire. Journalists who dragged his body off the road said he had been shot in the back, deliberately. Losers hate the press.

The war in Bosnia killed about sixty journalists, most of them, but not all, were local reporters and camera crews. Once a cosmopolitan world capital, Sarajevo became just another shithole, pummelled and bombed and beaten. A city of madmen surrounded by madmen. Getting in to cover the war was not easy. I was in Moscow working on a documentary when a frustrated call came from the CBC News desk in Toronto. Could I please help them get to Sarajevo? They had a crew sitting in Belgrade, unable or unwilling to risk going. When I met up with the four of them, they had been in the hotel a week and showed little inclination to move, but we finally drove to the Serb stronghold of Pale, and from there we would negotiate our way into Sarajevo.

The morning had come for us to go in. A Canadian UN armored convoy under the command of General Lewis MacKenzie was about to leave Pale, sprint across Sarajevo airport—possibly under enemy fire—and continue on to their HQ. We were invited to join them. At this moment, two of the CBC crew went berserk on me.

"I'm not going to spill my blood for the CBC! You just want to go because you like this sort of thing. I don't. I'm not dying for any broadcaster. I'm staying here."

"Well," I said, "I am going in. It's our job. That's why we're here."

The cameraman said he would go, too.

Eventually, the other two overcame their terror and joined us. However, one was so freaked by the fighting, she had to be confined to the hotel. The other blossomed into a very fine war correspondent. I've left out the names because I think they all have redeemed themselves since their hysterical display of fear.

In Sarajevo, we were filming one morning at a casualty aid station. Ambulances raced the wounded here first. Doctors and nurses rushed to the door every time one pulled up under a small canopy. But the ambulance bay was in the direct line of snipers in nearby hills, and their aim was deadly. Remember, some of them had been on the Olympic team. They had already killed several of the Samaritans. The Serb high command was said to be paying US$600 for a dead doctor, $500 for a dead nurse and about the same for a dead foreign journalist.

A boy about five was brought in bleeding from shrapnel wounds. An old woman, who had just been hit by a bullet, lay on a stretcher. The snipers were having a busy morning. We were just about to leave the aid station when a Bosnian soldier staggered in. He appeared drunk or high on drugs, and he was cradling a double-barreled shotgun. Suddenly, he rammed the gun into my stomach and pulled the trigger. It wasn't loaded, or at least it didn't go off. A joke, my friend. A joke.

It was not a joke when an aide to Yasser Arafat pulled a pistol on me. The Israelis had finally driven the Palestinian militias out of Beirut and into Syria. Arafat had gone days ago, but a few of his Fatah lieutenants stayed behind to clear out the chairman's office and destroy any incriminating or classified papers. They built a bonfire in the street outside the office in West Beirut and set ablaze a pile of papers and posters. Mike Sweeney filmed this symbolic end of the Palestinians as a force in Beirut and handed me the tape as he reloaded his camera. Just then, one of Arafat's men, a guy I had come to know quite well over my many visits to the building, stormed up to me.

"You have taken a picture of the chairman's face burning in the fire."

We hadn't because there wasn't a picture of Arafat to be seen anywhere, much to my disappointment.

"No we haven't. There are no pictures of the chairman on the fire."

"That is not true. One of my men saw you take a picture of the chairman. Hand over the tape please, Mr. John."

"Like I said, we did not take any pictures of the chairman because there weren't any."

"I want the tape."

"I'm sorry, I'm not going to give it to you."

That's when he pulled out the gun and pointed it at me.

"Give me the tape!"

A sane person would have complied, but I was so pissed off at this swaggering bully who thought he could control what went on TV, I went nuts.

"Who the fuck do you think you are? I told you we don't have any pictures of the chairman. Now put the gun away."

He lowered it but kept it pointed at me.

"Please, Mr. John, give me the tape."

"You are not getting the tape, but I'll make a deal with you. Let's go back to the hotel where we can screen the segment of the fire, and if there's a picture of the chairman you can have the tape. Deal?"

"Okay."

"But that's all I'm going to show you. That one segment. Deal?"

"Okay."

He kept the gun on his lap as we drove the twenty minutes back to the hotel. I kept the tape firmly clenched in my hands. At the hotel, I turned on the screening machine, fast-forwarded to the fire incident, and let the tape roll. No pictures of a flaming Arafat.

"See. I told you we didn't take any pictures of the chairman."

"Show me the rest of the tape, now."

"What? We had a deal. The deal was I would show you the

part with the fire. Nothing else. Okay?"

"I want to see the rest of the tape."

"You're not going to. We made a deal. I trusted you to stick by your word and now you're telling me you can't be trusted?"

"Okay. Let's go back."

Who was the stupider person here? Discuss.

13

Stars and Gripes

To help you with the discussion, let me introduce you to some of the more unkind terms we in television use to describe our assigned functions. The reporter is known as the lips or the spoon (those who have to be fed their lines). The camera operator, obviously, the eyes; the soundperson, the ears; and the producer? The asshole. And then there's the animal we call the Big Foot, the heavyweight, the star correspondent who is assigned to multi-country swings or the really big story, where he or she moves in on a bureau and walks over the resident reporter.

When Global Television went on air in Canada, there were no foreign bureaus, but the two anchormen, both called Peter, were assigned the big foreign stories. One took us to Paris with Prime Minister Pierre Trudeau, who engaged in huge amounts of pomp and not a lot else.

"Les Morts! Les Morts!" they shouted. The veterans of World Wars I and II wanted more war? Could this be possible? No, asshole, you've just stepped on the Tomb of the Unknown Soldier. *Sacre bleu! Qui? Moi?* Yes, you, asshole.

But my faux pas, well, paled compared with that of the esteemed and steaming Peter Big Foot. Well respected as a political reporter and columnist, a man of aplomb and an occasional plum, he spoke fluent French, was a patron of the arts, seldom farted and was generally much "couthed" and refined for one in our profession. The apogee, the peak, the pinnacle of the tour was a pilgrimage to the Sorbonne, the holiest shrine of scholarship in all Europe, although such a claim would be contested by Oxford, Cambridge and Neasden High. Trumpets sounded, the learned ones swished and swashed in their scarlet and gold robes, and Pierre accepted an honorary degree in Certain Things. It was an afternoon affair, and our Peter was overcome with emotion. To be in the Sorbonne amid scholastic deity; to see and feel the aestheticism, the culture, the grandeur. All else paled that memorable afternoon, including Peter. Very paled, ashen, in fact. A quick puffing of the cheeks and lurching of the stomach and out it came. Breakfast! Lunch! A nifty croissant, *boeuf au gratin*, lightly sautéed asparagus, *moules marinières*, Sorbonne sorbet, gateaux, tea, cognac, Chateau Mârgaux '66. A true gourmet throw-up. Resident professors scurried around, spooning it into paper bags to take home for *dejeuner*. And the word spread to the four corners of Paris ... the Sorbonne now has three stars in the Michelin guide; two for texture, one for aftertaste. We called it Big-Foot-in-mouth syndrome.

Now to Bonn, once a candidate for the most boring capital city in the world. It had fierce competition, though, from Ottawa, Brasilia and Singapore. (Bonn lost its capital status, but not all its federal government departments, to Berlin after German reunification in 1990.) Bonn is all gray and concrete and was on the itinerary of the same five-nation jaunt Pierre Trudeau took to Paris, London, Rome and Brussels. When news people travel with heads of state, we are herded to the back of the bus, plane, train, scooter or bicycle, and while the sirs are noshing quails' eggs, pâté and

Dom Perignon, the hacks at the back often decamp to their hotel rooms or TV stations to file their never-failingly tedious, spoon-fed "political analysis" stories. (February 1976 was the only time a Prime Ministerial trip gave the newsmen, but not necessarily all the newswomen, something to get a grip on. Margaret Trudeau turned up braless at a Pierre and Fidel rally in Cienfuegos, Cuba. She was wearing a Liberal Party T-shirt, and I could see her nipples straining for a better view of the Bearded One.)

Bonn was the stop before Rome on this particular odyssey into stupor, in which Trudeau was trying to promote his esoteric theory of a contractual link with the European Common Market. Exhausted, hung over and irritable, the press checked into the Hotel Steigenberger, a quick pit stop before whatever afternoon follies had been arranged.

"Hello, room service?"

"Jaa."

"Could I please have one chicken sandwich with no mayonnaise?"

"One chicken sandwich. What color bread do you want?"

"White."

"So that is one chicken sandwich on white bread. Is that correct?"

"Yes. But no mayonnaise."

"Jaa. Of course."

Knock, knock.

"Here's your sandwich, Herr Scully."

Herr today. Rome tomorrow.

Just one bite, that's all it took. The dreaded mayonnaise. In a fit of petulance, Herr-to-the-thrown hurled the sandwich out the window. Which was closed. It hit, mayo-side down.

In another German hotel I asked for coffee and toast and up came a chocolate cake.

In the Legend Inn, New Delhi, the cistern had sprung a leak and flooded the bathroom at 11:15 PM. The night manager sent up his "boy," who fixed it within seconds. And within seconds it became unfixed. Up came the night manager himself. He plunged his arm into the cistern and pushed and pulled and clearly had no idea what he was doing. And still the water flowed. I would have to wait until morning when the engineer would be on duty. No. It must be fixed tonight. It's going to flood the entire second floor!

"Okay, okay, I will send someone to fix it." Ten minutes later the room service waiter was at my door. He tried. No. He couldn't fix it either. Nothing could be done until morning. It was now midnight, but trying to please, he asked:

"Would you like to order dinner?"

Back in Germany it was federal election time. Herr-we-go-again. I flew from Toronto to join the crew and correspondent from Paris. I checked into the Frankfurt Intercontinental and phoned Marsha, the local freelancer I had hired to translate and handle hotels, transport and satellite feed points. Yes, she had ordered the eight-seater minibus for the morning and it would be outside the hotel at 8:45 AM. Come the morn, the only buses there were six huge tourist coaches, the ones with personal video screen, leather seats and luxury lavatories.

"Where's the minibus, Marsha?"

"In the car park. The driver apologized for being late. Come, John, I'll show you."

I still couldn't see the minibus.

"There, John. That's the bus."

A massive, gleaming tourist behemoth with fifty seats for the CBC, all five of us.

"They didn't have a smaller one."

Still, it might have been worse. She could have turned up with a mayonnaise chocolate cake.

On an earlier trip to Germany, we were covering the "notorious autumn" of violence by extremists from the Red Army Faction, also known as the Baader-Meinhoff Gang. The self-styled urban terrorists had killed over thirty German officials, chauffeurs and bodyguards. Then, in one forty-eight-hour period, they killed a pilot while hijacking a Lufthansa flight to Somalia, and local cops found industrialist Hanns-Martin Schleyer executed and stuffed into the trunk of a green Audi. It was around 6:00 PM on a somber, drizzling night, a night during which two imprisoned gang members would commit suicide.

Toronto wanted us to satellite them the story. Using German footage and our own, plus a piece to camera by our reporter, Dale Goldhawk, we fed out of ARD studios in Cologne. The American network, ABC, was also there, feeding first. They were helpful to us and generous with the satellite time, encouraged to do so by a correspondent who said he was a Canadian. Peter Jennings. Never heard of him.

Next morning, Germany awoke to the realization that something terrible was again haunting the nation still trying to bury its past. Police and Special Forces swamped the area. They set up roadblocks and checked identities as helicopters clattered and swooped overhead in search of their prey. Our follow-up story was going to include a segment of the effects of the terrorism on

Germany's surging economy. From the autobahn between Cologne and the airport you could see a major chemical plant, a symbol of the rejuvenated country. As we drove along, camera-man Reg Thomas took a tracking shot of the plant, but he wasn't happy with it so we got off at the next exit, turned around and did the shot again. Then we headed back toward Bonn for a couple of interviews and to get footage of the extraordinary security measures being taken around the Bundestag (Parliament), including armored cars and infantry soldiers with heavy weapons. This was a country again at war. But we never got there.

The first unusual noise we noticed was a helicopter. It was right above us. I mean like a few meters above us, hovering over our car. Two police cars screamed up behind us, one sliced in front and we were trapped. Shit-scared, too. No one was kidding in Germany this morning. Did they think we were terrorists?

"Out! Out!" One didn't need to speak fluent German to get their drift, or miss the sight of a gun barrel aimed straight at us.

"Passports!"

"So you are Canadians," observed the senior cop, who switched into English.

"What were you doing driving up and down the autobahn photographing the chemical plant?"

They thought we were on a reconnaissance mission, possibly planning to blow it up.

We explained that we were a TV crew and showed them our German press credentials and our gear.

"Okay. But next time, you tell us. You could have been in a lot of trouble. We were going to shoot your car."

Flughafen, bitte. (Airport, please.) And make it pretty *schnell*.

14

Boys Behaving Terribly

Not all television crews spend their time racing around the globe, theorizing on Islamic fundamentalism or the causes of violence. Some of our work is quite mundane—well, dead boring. Take this next scene, for example:

Millhaven Maximum Penitentiary, Kingston, Ontario. It is a forbidding place and houses some of Canada's toughest criminals. The prison is like most modern jails: low slung, gray, perimeter fences, cameras, floodlights, guard towers, a vast parking lot and nothing else for miles. A bleak and desolate place. Although they have brightened it a bit recently by erecting a special block to prove that Canada is one of the great liberal democracies that has the utmost respect for the law and justice. This is where they hold suspected terrorists without trial, without ever seeing the evidence against them. It is dubbed "Guantanamo North."

We were there to cover a news story involving Millhaven's guards. A fact-finding committee went into the prison that morning to investigate complaints about working conditions. Our brief was to get pictures and interviews with them and also with the prison guards as they left at the end of their shifts. It was the middle of winter, with the temperature well below freezing. Prison officials would not let us wait inside, so we sat in the car with the engine running to keep warm. The cameraman, Alan Fung, was a recent arrival from Hong Kong. He was very good at his job but still not too fluent in English. After we had waited in the parking lot for a couple of hours, the steel gates clanked open and a group of guards walked toward us. Out we got, camera rolling. Reporter Tony Hillman asked three or four incisive questions, got a few usable clips, and we got back into the car, where Alan asked: "Did you want sound with those interviews?"

No one would tell us how long the fact-finders would be in the prison or when they would be leaving, so we settled in for a long wait, still a bit perturbed at our silent interviews. An hour passed, then two. We were bored rigid. Alan announced he had to pee. No, the prison would not let him use their facilities; there were no shrubs, bushes, rocks or anything else to give him cover from the guard tower. Then one of us had the very good idea to open the trunk and use it to block anyone's view. Round the back of the car went Alan. We popped the trunk. Al unzipped, flipped it out and started his own jet stream.

As alluded to earlier, the children in the car were bored. The engine was running, so one of us slipped the gear into drive and the car took off with Al desperately running behind, still peeing but now spraying in all directions. We stopped about twenty meters later.

What's that saying about the devil finding work for idle hands?

A few years later, Tony Hillman would pay for that prank— of course, it was Tony who put the gear into drive—when he and two CBC TV colleagues were trying to get from Toronto to a big story (civil war, earthquake, mass graves) in Central America. As usual, they were in a hurry, but arrived in Miami to find all flights to their destination canceled. But being resourceful lads, they managed to find a charter company willing to fly them. It was night and the weather was terrible, slashing rain and wind. But the two pilots were sure they could get through the storm. The plane was a small, propeller-driven, four-passenger aircraft, with the two flyboys up front.

Mike Sweeney, Alister Bell and Tony had brought all the essential supplies along, together with some camera gear. The essential supplies were vodka and orange juice. But what our much-traveled heroes forgot was that small planes do not have toilets. They demolished the vodka and orange remarkably swiftly, and just as swiftly their bladders filled to bursting point. Desperate, one of them came up with an inspired solution. They could pee into the empty bottles! Our first hero adroitly almost filled the first bottle. Next hero's turn. Out came the amber liquid, just as the plane hit an air pocket—Whaao! All over the pilots and their windshield.

"Damn!" said the senior pilot. "This plane's leaking! We'll get it checked as soon as we land."

Not just camera crews get caught with their flies open or their pants down.

It is three in the morning. Boom! Boom! Boom! Not artillery starting another civil war, but a bass drum. In El Salvador, every town has a week-long festival to mark the birthday of its patron saint, Fiestas Patronales. In the town of Ilabasco it starts on September 29, the birthday of St. Miguel. People from across the region flock to Ilabasco. There are parades, floats, marching girls, arts, crafts, food stalls, a Ferris wheel, all accompanied by fireworks that bang and splutter all day and all night long. It's not a great time to catch up on some sleep. But the festival gives the townsfolk a sticky and stinky problem. All those out-of-towners at some time have to have an "evacuation"—it means the same in Spanish or English—a dump. And there are no Port-a-Loos. Being modest, the dumpers look for cover, which they find in sheltered doorsteps where they squat, drop, dump and run. Instead of a welcome mat, the owner of the house gets a welcome splat from their strangers in the night, exchanging glances over a pile of shite. "Enough!" said the homeowners. What kind of a dump do you think this is?

Now, every night during Fiestas Patronales, the house owners hide. When they espy a dumper, on go the taps; jets of water fly out of the hoses and hit the squatter in mid-dump. Shrieks and a terrible choice: finish, or shit and run, pants still entangled with ankles, praying that everything else gets left behind.

It fixed the problem this year but there's always next time.

→■● ●■←

"Now, you all wait out here. I don't want you people stealing anything."

"But we have to go in and set up our equipment for the interview."

"Well, just don't steal anything."

The trusting, generous host was the president of Israel, Chaim Herzog. His palatial mansion befitted a man of his self-imagined stature, former Israeli Ambassador to the UN, former resistance fighter, former London barrister, professional asshole, born in

Northern Ireland in 1921, the same year the IRA drove the Brits out of the South. In hindsight, it was a great pity they didn't move further north and drive assholes out, too, even if they were still wetting their diapers.

Apart from being told we were potential thieves, Herzog demanded we leave our shoes and coats in his vast lobby because he did not want us bringing any dirt into his house. We were not offered the usual courtesies of food or drink or a modicum of respect. So why did he let the CBC into his opulent oasis? Because egomaniacs can never resist being on television. If the price is to endure thieves like us, then so be it. But his face, he, would be seen and he'd be even more famous and even greater than anyone could possibly imagine. I recall little of the interview except for its fascistic, shallow and short-sighted views on the region. But I do remember clearly that when the interview was over, he warned us he was watching, and he stood and stared until the potential pilferers left.

Such a nice man. He died in 1993. Oooh.

But Herzog had a point. Not about stealing; but TV crews are dangerous. The moment we walk into the room, we start re-arranging, disassembling and occasionally breaking objects, moving your world around so our cumbersome paraphernalia of lights, cables, tripods and people can fit into our idea of how the room should be set for a TV interview. We've overloaded circuits and blown fuses in houses, churches, halls and, once, an entire village in Russia.

But there is one incident I only now feel comfortable talking about. I don't think anyone will come after us after all this time, will they? It was 1981 and we were in the home of the father of the Lebanese Phalange Party, the patrician, rich, aristocratic Christian leader, Pierre Gemayel. The décor was exquisite. Louis XV furniture, chandeliers, rich carpets, fabulous tapestries; oak and mahogany abounded, as did deep reds and muted hues. This was before Beirut bombs did some re-arranging of their own and, in the process, killed three male members of his family dynasty.

Mr. Gemayel was almost indifferent to our presence, but polite and not unwelcoming.

We decided to set up our equipment for the interview in his breathtakingly adorned main living room. This process can take anywhere from ten minutes to an hour, depending on the complexity of the light and the type of shot the producer wants. The crew finished lighting in about forty minutes and we were about to call Mr. Gemayel back into the room, when reporter Linden MacIntyre and I smelled something unusual. Was something burning? No? Yeah, there is. Fuck, I can smell it!

Jeezus Christ! It's that Louis Quinze chair! There's smoke coming from it! Little curls and wisps, not billowing belching clouds, but smoke just the same. Fuck, he'll kill us!

I won't divulge the identity of the soundman who dropped his cigarette on the chair and set it afire, because his name is Alister Bell.

We frantically smacked the chair into submission and frenetically fanned the air, willing it to head in the direction of an open window. Back at the chair, a small, cigarette-sized hole had emerged as the sum total of the damage, but if Gemayel saw or smelled anything, we'd all be inducted into his Balls of Fame.

We moved the incendiary piece of furniture to the back of the room, and just to make sure, I sat on it throughout Mr. Gemayel's entire presence. He left us alone to pack up. Then we left, almost at a sprint. Sure, it was a cowardly thing to do. And what would you have done?

→■● ●■←

"You're having a great time wherever you are. You're the life of the party."

Who are we talking about here? Virgo. It's a horoscope for one of the great comedy routines of all time, the Virgo (true) Mother Teresa. Albanian-born Agnes Gonxha Bojaxhiu would have been ninety-seven on August 26, 2007. But she died ten years ago, so wasn't.

I met Aggie, this saint-on-earth, in Calcutta where she was running her orphanages. She was also cultivating a celebrity image. That meant treating us scum of the press with contempt as she went about her godly duties of greeting more important guests … the ones who had much more money to donate to her good works. There are scurrilous stories that she siphoned off a lot for herself. I have no proof whatsoever of this, but it would explain her fits of depression and doubts about the existence of the very God to whom she was so overtly devoted. She was also reported to have said she was not interested in the poor but only in spreading the power of the Catholic Church around the world. This, too, is in dispute, even today.

She won the Nobel Peace Prize in 1979. I guess it was for creating the same kind of peace as other great winners of the vaunted prize: Henry Kissinger, F.W. de Klerk, Yasser Arafat and Yitzhak Rabin.

After she died, the besotted reactionary, Pope John Paul II, went on a beatification bender, sending nearly thirteen hundred souls on the second step to sainthood, including Albanian Aggie, who is about to set a record for the fastest canonization in the church's history. Why the rush? Well, they don't want the rumors and doubts to be true, do they? That would really make monkeys out of men who insist their papacy makes them infallible. Except when they are wrong. So let's declare her a saint, ASAP.

So I hope Aggie is having a great time on her birthday. Even Virgos, modest and shy, gotta have fun in this life, or the next. If there is a next. Otherwise, Aggie fooled us all.

Someone else who has fooled many of us is Phil the Greek. The imperious, racist husband of Betty, Queen of England. His improper title is Duke of Edinburgh. He's the guy who warned a group of British kids in China that if they stayed there too long they'd all get "slitty-eyed."

This fine fellow is also known for his pathological hatred of the media, a trait, along with secret nocturnal humping, he has passed on to his genius of a son, Prince Charles. It was dopey Chas who was caught by a new type of ultrasensitive parabolic microphone used by the BBC. The scene was a so-called photo opportunity for the usual inane occasion—a birthday, a divorce, a beheading. The animals of the press were kept behind a rope perhaps ten meters from Chas and his spring-offs. The animals had to shout their questions and hope to catch a usable reply, which is not easy when dealing with an intellectual capacity as large as that borne by all that Chas. A BBC reporter had the audacity to ask a question that had a semblance of relevance to it.

Chas, thinking no one could hear him, turned to one of his

kin and whispered for the entire world to hear:

"God, I hate that man. I can't stand him." Sheer brilliance. But then, he had a great teacher, his equally brilliant father.

I remember covering Phil and Betty on one of their deeply rewarding and meaningful trips to Canada. We were in Kingston, Ontario.

We had decided that the reporter, David Burt, would do an on-camera that day. But David had just received a nasty surprise in a brown paper package. The hotel laundry had shrunk his safari suit so badly, it was too tight to wear. So he borrowed a pair of scissors and begun cutting the stitches in the suit. First to go, the stitching that was holding up the hems and cuffs. A quick run over with an iron would hide the crease marks, and the sleeves and trousers would be long enough to be sartorially acceptable. Then he attacked another part of the jacket, making slits under the arms so it would fit his bulky frame. Next target for the boy with the bulge was the trousers' crotch. I watched with only vague amusement. I was disconcerted by the day's itinerary. What in the hell can we do with this load of rubbish to make the royal tour even remotely interesting? They were going to do a walkabout and then have lunch with a group of seniors or wankers or whomever.

Same old dreary shit.

I was stirred from my musing by an increasingly uncomfortable feeling as David hacked away at the safari suit.

"Fuck the laundry. Jeezus! I'll fucking kill them. Fuck!"

"Um, David. What size is that suit?"

"What do you mean?"

"What size is it?"

"Well, it was 'Large' before the fucking laundry got hold of it."

"Check the label."

"Huh? How the fuck did that happen? It says 'Medium.'"

"David, I think you've just ripped *my* safari suit to pieces."

Yep. We had bought identical safari suits, identical color, and didn't tell each other. Now we had one suit between the two of us.

Royal walkabouts defy logic. Betty walks two paces ahead of Phil. Betty clutches a posy proffered to her by some curtsying kid, who just happens to be the daughter of the mayor or other local huge-head. Then, flag-waving idolaters shout and sing, "God Save the Queen"—a chant more apposite now in places of gay abandon than in colonialist street theater.

But this was the job and we had to do it. The walkabouts are strictly controlled so that no one can actually, heaven forbid, touch these demi-, well, semi- as in tractor-trailer, Gods. I thought we might get a better shot of this nonsense if we ducked under the ropes and went over to the other side. Film purists will say I've just crossed the axis, not of evil, but of angle. Trust me, on this day I didn't give a damn.

But that meant also crossing the forbidden path of wanker Phil.

"Get out of the bloody way. I should have you buggers arrested," was his kind and understanding response to our desire to get better pictures of him and his loathsome dove.

15

The Sands of Terror

"Not bad for a sixty-seven-year-old" beamed the ebullient John Bierman (of BBC *Bloody Sunday* fame). We were in a bar on Church Street in Toronto and all was well in John's world after the publisher accepted his latest book, *Dark Safari*. In a couple of years he would retire to Cyprus, now that it had settled down and the UN had successfully kept the Greeks and the Turks apart. It was a very different Cyprus from the one the Turks invaded in 1975. Then there were many casualties, not all of them military. Two were BBC colleagues, Ted Stoddard soundman, and reporter Simon Dring. The crew stopped their car on a road that could have been mined, and they peered through the windshield looking for the telltale signs of lumps of disturbed earth or bitumen. Ted wanted to take a closer look. He stepped out of the car, right on top of a landmine, and was blown to pieces. Dring was seriously injured but still managed to do a piece to camera as blood poured down his face. The cameraman, Keith Skinner, was not physically hurt.

In Uganda, our CBC *Journal* crew had driven three nasty hours along mud-holed roads, snaking through the jungle to reach a refugee center set up to protect those fleeing the guerrilla war. Idi Amin and his heads-in-the-fridge brigade had gone, to be eventually replaced by Yoweri Museveni, who now had to fight the appallingly brutal and mad men from the Lord's Resistance Army. Methinks the Lord will have just two words to say to the LRA for using his name in vain when they finally meet up, and the last word will be "off!"

We taped at the camp for an hour. Refugee camps never vary. They are always squalid, filthy, smoky and strewn with piles of excrement. The refugees are always afraid, tearful, hurt, damaged, dehumanized, either freezing cold or sweltering hot; many are sick, coughing, vomiting and dying. And yet, someone in the camp always finds a glass of tea and a chair to try to make the visitor feel welcome. Their dignity and goodness amid such repugnance can be gut-wrenching.

As we left the camp, an aid worker told our Ugandan driver and his mechanic of a much quicker way back to the capital, Kampala.

"Take this road for a mile, turn left and you'll be on the highway."

Hugely relieved, they followed his instructions. Just as the minivan reached the highway, a soldier waved his gun and ordered us to stop, but all he wanted was a lift up the road, and about a kilometer further on, he got out and waved goodbye. The van carried along the highway, but something was wrong. There was no other traffic, no cyclists and no pedestrians. The road was deserted. It had been mined. Landmines are usually buried just below the surface. They are now often called "explosive improvised devices" or IEDs, especially when they're homemade, as in the camps of Afghanistan or the back rooms of Iraq or Iran. When a vehicle or person comes into contact, the mine explodes, and deadly fragments shoot out at high speeds. It's estimated there are over a one hundred million landmines in seventy countries. Since 1975, landmines have killed or maimed more than one million people. Turning back *now* wouldn't help. We had unwittingly avoided driving over a landmine so far, but chance it again? The only thing to do was to slow the hired minibus to a crawl. Inside, no one said a word. The two Ugandans broke into a sweat as they leaned and craned over the dashboard, searching for any disturbed mounds before a wheel rolled over them. There's one! Stop! Inch around. Careful! Careful! Inch around. Just the one, unless more were better buried. If they were, we did not hit them, and finally made it out safely.

The point I am making here is that if you are ever tempted to open a rental car business, *never* rent anything to a TV crew. And that brings us back to the Turkish invasion of Cyprus. Mike Sweeney and Don North had managed to find one of the few rental cars not already hired by the international media. When they left Cyprus, they did a favor for a TV reporter from a rival network and handed the car over to him. Fast forward to the Global Television Newsroom in Toronto two months later.

"Where's our car?"

"What car?"

"The one you rented in Cyprus. Where is it?"

"In Cyprus, where we left it."

The long-distance caller was becoming agitated.

"Where did you leave it?"

"In Cyprus, with a colleague."

"But you didn't tell us. Where did your colleague leave the car?"

"I don't know."

"Well, you'd better find out. Your name is on the rental agreement and you are responsible. If you can't tell me where the car is, you will have to pay for it. All of it."

That came to $15,000.

Frantic phone calls to faraway places.

"What happened to the car? … It was what?!"

Hit by an artillery shell. Boom. No more car. The reporter was not in it at the time.

"Jeezuz, they're going to bill us for $15,000!"

"Oooh, sorry about that, pardner."

So, what did the lads do? After much sweating, begging and pleading, they wriggled away, thanks to a genius of an accountant and an understanding insurance company. An understanding insurance company? Well, maybe a penny or two did change hands.

They won't do that again, will they?

The boys got off lightly. In war zones now, you hire high-powered, armor-plated SUVs worth around $150,000. A common old non-war-zone supercharged Range Rover will set the owner back about a hundred grand. Those are ones a mom uses to pick up her one kid after school, fueling the economy and the want, not the need. Our need was for something a little cheaper when we landed in Mali, the former French colony in northeast Africa. It is a hot, dusty, sandy, developing nation whose one tourist attraction is Timbuktu. It really exists. Our need in Mali was also for a Land Rover. Well, it started out as a Land Rover we hired from Smert Cars in Bamako, the capital. With the vehicle came a driver, a mechanic, and at various times across the Sahara, a guide.

The TV documentary was to be about desertification, the

spreading south of the mighty Sahara, as it turned rivers into sand, forests into twigs, choked life out of local economies and threatened the existence of tens of thousands of nomadic tribesmen and their families. Climate change caused by global warming.

Although Timbuktu has an airstrip, we drove the roughly one thousand kilometers, since parts of the story were in settlements en route. We guessed we would take three days and nights to get there, spend three or four days taping, and then drive back to Bamako.

The boys from Smert drove their Land Rover up to the parking lot of the Hotel Sofitel l'Amité for inspection. The vehicle was way too small. It would never carry six people, half a dozen camera equipment cases as well as food and drink (mainly cases of Heineken and fewer bottles of water). Could you fit on a roof rack? *Oui.* How long would this take? By the morning? Great.

As promised, the Land Rover appeared the next morning with its rooftop appendage. We loaded the camera cases onto the new roof rack, tied everything down with rope, and off we set for Timbuktu, three and four. Five minutes after our triumphal departure, the Land Rover conked out. Dead.

"Too much weight!" cried the driver. "Too much weight! We leave boxes behind."

Not a bad idea. We could drive through sandstorms, cross the Sahara, sweat and choke for five days, and then turn around and come back without any pictures. I thought it was brilliant but Mike Sweeney had a better idea.

"Why don't we put some gas in the tank. It's empty."

The smart Smert boys hadn't thought of that.

Ten hours later, our first major stop was the desert town of

Gao, where we checked into the no-star Seef of the Sahara. It was filthy and swarmed with thirsty mosquitoes, since there was no running water. The stench came from other dwellers and a thousand camels that, for centuries, plodded defiantly along the fabled caravan routes laden with gold, spices, salt and tapestries. The suffocating heat of the day slopped into the suffocating heat of night. The "hotel" had no fans, no air-conditioning, and mere drops of water dripping from slime-encrusted, rusted taps.

The mattresses were draped in mosquito nets a hippopotamus could fly through. What, they don't have wings? Damn! Fooled again.

Gao is a town of refugees, mainly Tuareg nomads fleeing the invading sands. Gao also has a camel fair and the wonderful dung beetle. Guess how it got its name? Yes! Eating dung—wonderful dung from camels, dogs, cows, sheep, rats, yetis, grizzlies, lions, tigers, monkeys, rhinoceroses, pigs, buffalo and animals of that nature.

Gao awoke early. By 6:00 AM the town was jumping: kids off to school and shop shutters opened as a sizeable number of the townsfolk took their morning dump by the side of the road, as the dung beetles blissfully sang and danced cheek to cheek.

Five hours later, Gao died. The cauldron heat and the drenching humidity turned breathing into gasping at 45°C. No one ventured out again until late afternoon. We taped the refugees, a bit of Gao life and the wood police. The what? The wood police. They were conducting a war, not on drugs, not on Islam (that would be silly, since most were Muslim) not on terror, but a War on Wood. So much fertile land had been lost to the Sahara that trees and their wood were more valuable than gold. The wood police patrolled the town and pounced on anyone who seemed to have too much. Where did you get it? How much did you pay for it? Don't you know we're trying to save the trees? When it came to wood, they were only trying to save themselves.

One more night in the Sahara Seef and then we were off into the desert headed for Timbukfive. The roof rack seemed to have loosened a little; the welding may not have been thorough enough, but the Smert Two reckoned it was okay. There are no roads in the desert, no signposts, traffic lights, cops or gas stations, just undulating sand, stones and scrub, and a "local" to guide us past his own particular pile of sand. The Land Rover slammed over sand-covered rocks, plunged down a sand hill, got stuck, pushed out and pushed on. Then we heard a scraping noise over our heads. The roof rack! The joints were getting looser, but not enough to cause any panic. We tied the equipment down more securely and bumped and slewed our way in the general direction of Timbuksix.

Barely ten minutes later came a massive grinding noise, then a tearing, and then the roof rack and one hundred kilograms of gear catapulted off the roof and crashed onto the hood. Catastrophe. The joints had ripped open and left glistening, gaping holes. Hmmm. None of us had the number of the local Automobile Association and our professional lives flashed before our eyes, as in finished, dead in the sand, you might say. Then, seemingly out of nowhere, twenty or so nomadic men, women and children appeared over a sand ridge, and they looked and looked and looked at the men and woman from Mars with the strangely colored skin. Surmising that none of them had a degree in mechanical engineering, we enjoined them to fuck off, but they didn't. They stayed and sat and stared.

So, what do we do now? And "now" was not long before

sunset. Oh, joy, a night in the desert. Each of us witty boys and a girl had very different but very practical solutions to our problem. Al Bell thought if we drank all the Heineken we could pack up our troubles in our old kit bags and smile, smile, smile. Mike Sweeney suggested cyanide pills, but then Toronto would have no one to give shit to for wrecking a Land Rover and leaving $100,000 worth of gear in the Sahara. I suggested self-immolation, knowing full well that Ann Medina would never, ever give up her lighter fluid, not one puff's worth. Hara-kiri? Or even Bert-kiri? Nope. Too messy and our knives were probably not sharp enough.

Meanwhile, the Smert boys were in a quandary of their own. If they brought the Land Rover back half ripped open, their boss would rip them half open, but if they left it in the desert, they would be in even deeper trouble. Motivated by fear of the loss of their very personal male belongings, they got to work, removed the gear, slid the rack back on top, and then lashed it to other parts of the vehicle, re-loaded the equipment, lashed that too and prayed to Allah.

It was dark now. Nothing to do but to endorse Al's suggestion about the beer, eat tinned meat, a bottle of Medina's olives and sleep under the stars. Contrary to what the guidebooks say, the Sahara is not frigid at night, at least not this night. It was warm and silent.

At sunrise, we made a quick check of the roof rack, and moved off toward Timbukseven, very slowly. Minutes later the rack began to groan, as did those underneath it. If it shot off again, we would have to ditch the gear or lie stranded in the Sahara. Slowly, slowly the Smertmobile inched ahead, until there in the distance was the legendary Timbukeight. In the fifteenth century, it was queen of the desert, a rich Muslim city with a population of a hundred thousand; now it has only forty thousand. It is brown and drab, a market and an ordinary but functioning hotel. The most fascinating part was the river where the boats had plied their trades, tying up at the market jetty and unloading fish and figs and sweetmeats and fresh vegetables. Not any more. It's all sand now. There is no water for miles.

Our next problem was how to get back to Bamako with the gear. The Smertmobile was not an option, but there was that landing strip! And sitting in the capital was a charter plane that came and took the CBC Four away while the Smert Two had a nasty four-day trip back.

They stormed into the hotel. Yes, their boss was really unhappy with the condition of his Land Rover and he wanted $1,000 for repairs. We opined that it was his lads who had installed the roof rack and they knew we were going to Timbuknine. They knew the weight of the equipment, so, sorry, *mes amis*, you are not getting one single franc. And they didn't.

Never rent a vehicle to a TV crew.

Before we left Mali, we saw attempts by various international agencies to improve agricultural growth and, impossibly, stop the desert. Mali is now one of the poorest countries on earth, with an average income of just $900. Life expectancy is half that of wealthier countries; one hundred and forty thousand people have HIV/AIDS; Mali is dependent on its cotton exports, but crippling subsidies by richer countries, particularly the U.S., guarantee a future of hardship and poverty.

16

Terror's End

Poverty is the cause of most of the world's iniquities, and therefore the basis of most of the world's problems. Until poverty is assaulted and eradicated, cultural and religious bigotry annihilated, the way ahead will get grimmer.

Consider this: Over a million children die every year because they don't have clean drinking water and sanitation. I've seen them in slums around the world, drinking, washing and defecating in the same water because that's all they have. Eleven million will die before their fifth birthday ... one-fifth from diarrhea. They and their families are deprived of the basic requirements for human life, food, shelter and water. Yet while the West embarks on admirable offensives against AIDS and breast cancer, for example, it neglects the simplest, yet least glamorous and most far-off of curable diseases, poverty. We are outraged that there are eleven million child laborers in India alone, and we launch a campaign to stop it. Yet how many stop to think why the scourge of child labor exists. Half a billion Indians live in poverty; if the children do not go out to work, their families die.

In Rwanda, 60 percent live below the poverty line. In South Africa it's 50 percent, in Sudan 40 percent. By comparison, the figures for Australia and New Zealand are so low they are not applicable. And like the boat people from Vietnam, the poor of Africa risk their lives trying to escape to Europe by the hundreds every day. The few that survive the scorching, thirst-driven sea journey often land in Italy, Spain or Malta, are fed, jailed or sent back; few are given asylum. Imagine their disbelief if they were swept ashore in the French Riviera. For they would not understand one man's apogee of self-indulgence: a $200 million yacht, with its own submarine and helicopter. The vessel is over one hundred meters long and belongs to a billionaire industrialist. Does he need the yacht? No. Does he want it? Yes. Thereby hangs the difference between the haves and the have-nots; we want, we buy or we take. Those who need, wait or die. If the billionaire were to realize that it costs fourteen cents only to feed a child dying of hunger in Zimbabwe, or a buck a week, he could feed, clothe, house and educate it and hundreds of others for the rest of their lives just by hocking his yacht. But that isn't going to happen. Rich boys want rich toys and status symbols that tell us their impossible wealth proves they are better than us, and certainly better than the poverty-stricken wretches who now number a billion.

Yachting has a repugnant way of differentiating between them and us, like the professional golfer earning even more money from sports shirts and shoes. We subconsciously flaunt our apparel that says we are better than the poor, who probably made that T-shirt or running shoe or iPod in overcrowded, choking sweatshops in Central America or Asia for cents a day.

Only the super-rich and their consciences can afford to indulge in one of Western sports most craven, materialistic pastimes, the America's Cup, in which millions are invested to win bragging rights and yachting's greatest prize, until recently, the

LouisVuitton Cup.The race is spectacular to watch but a depraved use of wealth. I got to know the America's Cup intimately, and nothing about it was pretty. Here's why.

There comes a time in a young lad's life when his fancy turns to other pastures. Time to hand the baton on to even younger Turks who are yelping at the rungs of the ladder to success. Nipping at the heels. Dogging the footsteps.

The urinal at the Ramada Inn on College Street, Toronto, is not where one expects to piss away one's career. The dregs of a *Journal* Christmas party, sure, but a whole career? Big, burly Kiwi Ross Kenwood chose this moment to unburden himself on his fellow urinator. He also talked.

"D'ya know TVNZ is looking for a head of current affairs?"

"Why? Has he gone missing?"

"Asshole! No, mate, they want a new one."

"Why are you telling me this?"

"Well, sport, mate, cobber, fuckwit, I thought you might be interested."

TVNZ, an acronym to bring tears to the eyes of hardened newsmen and newswomen: Television New Zealand. The public broadcaster in a country with a population of four million, mainly white, middle class, and an indigenous Maori population of just over half a million. In fact, the Maori name for New Zealand is Aotearoa, the Land of the Long White Cloud, perhaps more aptly, the Land of the Long White Shroud. Peter Ustinov went there one day, but it was closed.

I had been back to my native New Zealand a number of times with fond memories. Like the time I was accosted on a Wellington street by a total stranger and told to get a bloody haircut (my locks were fashionably lovely at the time, hanging in blond swoops down to my shoulders). News executives told me after I suggested they run some pictures on their evening newscasts not to bring any of my foreign ideas here, mate. And autocue! Autocue. That's so phoney, mate. Our listeners like to see the top of the head of the bloke who's reading. And, no, we don't think sound has anything to do with TV. If we want sound we use some nice music. And still I went back to be head of current affairs.

"And wear a suit! And a tie! You can't dress like a hippie! And get your hair cut."

"Yes, mum." My dad, Ben Scully, had died several years earlier. He was a lawyer, a senior magistrate, then chief justice of Western Samoa and honored by the Queen. He was an important man with a fearsome reputation for vigorous jail sentences. I grew up not as John, but as "Ben's son." But with some chagrin, and I hope, hidden delight, he told me about a recent occasion when he was introduced to a journalists' convention: "Ladies and gentlemen, it's my great honor now to introduce our guest speaker, John's father, Mr. Ben Scully."

So I traveled to Avalon. Not whistling the Benny Goodman version of the jaunty old pop song. But to another Avalon, not too far from another bay, Wellington Harbour. But this Avalon was a gray, squat misery of a ten-story slab of concrete where TVNZ brass did their finest thinking. Me included. The Flying Squad! What a great idea. We would create a hit team of our best television news and current affairs journalists, producers and crews who would fly into action the moment a big story broke and produce an "instant" documentary. Everybody loved the idea. Sheer genius!

Other organizations had been doing it for years, but this was one "foreign idea" they loved.

The unit was formed amid great fanfare in December, when nothing happens except steaming hot midday Christmas dinner in high summer. But this year there was a story. And a *sports* story, to boot. Well, to sail. The America's Cup was being contested off the western coast of Australia, and New Zealand looked like winning! In sports-mad Kiwi land, World War Three could have been declared and the story would have been buried at the bottom of the news program, if it were run at all. The obsession with winning the Cup was so great that pilots on Air New Zealand domestic and international flights gave race updates every few minutes: "Good afternoon again, ladies and gentlemen, boys and girls. They're rounding the second buoy and *Stars and Stripes* is a boat length ahead. I'll get back to you just as soon as we get some more news up here on the flight deck."

Despite operating in a mainly Christian country, Air New Zealand domestic service is quite Islamic. Oh dear, no booze. But on one flight, a beefy lad next to me asked for "Mook Ploz." "Mook" as in "look." Mook Ploz. Was this the code to a secret stash of Steinlager? Mook Ploz? Hmm. I'd just have to wait for the flight attendant to return. She handed him a glass full of what looked like a very cold white liquid. This was Mook Ploz? It looked just like … wait a minute. I've seen that stuff before. It's milk! Many New Zealanders enunciate like frozen-faced dental patients for whom the anaesthetic never wears off. They don't move their mouths, lips or tongues. He wanted "milk, please."

Meanwhile, back at the America's Cup.

"The captain again, ladies and gentlemen, boys and girls. The two boats are engaged in a fierce tacking duel as they head down the course, and Chris Dixon and the Kiwis are fighting back. They've now gone half a boat length ahead."

Planes landed and passengers headed not to the baggage carousels but to TV sets in airports all over the country. The streets were even more deserted than usual. But the TV coverage seldom went beyond the Cup course. When it did, it was merely to show the crews getting on or off their boats. So I called in the Flying Squad. Their brief was to get the human drama behind the scenes, capture the tension and emotion. Get in with the crews and stay with them long before and long after the races were over. See and hear the hurt, the humiliation, the joy and elation. Wives, girlfriends, dinners, breakfasts.

The Flying Squad was to make the five-thousand-kilometer flight from Wellington to Perth, shoot for three days, edit in Perth for two days, and satellite the "instant documentary" back to New Zealand for broadcast at 7:00 PM, Sunday, the night before a critical race. TVNZ cleared its schedule for the documentary. It was Priority One. Nothing must get in its way. I appointed a senior producer to stay in Wellington to supervise the project, take care of all the logistics and facilities needed at our end. I was going to send a second producer to supplement the team in Perth, but the squad's producer assured me that wasn't necessary. He had everything in hand (he was in bed at the time).

The progress reports from our team were good. They were having trouble getting complete access to the behind-the-scenes drama, but they were confident of producing a first-class piece. On Saturday, the squad producer phoned to say they had begun editing, had great material and everything was looking just fine. The Flying Squad's debut would be spectacular, and I passed the good news on to my superiors. On Sunday morning at 4:30 AM (11:30 PM Saturday in Perth), the squad producer phoned again just to reaffirm that all was fine and they would edit through the night, which is normal for this kind of documentary.

The next day dawned warm but blustery in windy Wellington. The Sunday papers were full of America's Cup stories and pictures, but none of the print nor radio reporters had any of the emotion or drama Kiwis would be seeing on their TV screens in a few hours' time. After eight turbulent months as head of current affairs, I finally began to feel it was all coming together. Our standards were higher now, the journalism was better and the current affairs programs were much more aggressive. At six o'clock that evening, I poured myself a beer and waited for the moment of triumph. The news, of course, ran a Cup story and yet again reminded viewers of the feast to come in just under an hour's time.

At 6:40 PM my phone rang. It was Mark Westmoreland, the Wellington senior producer. The satellite had been booked to pre-record the documentary at 6:15 PM.

"John, they're not going to make it."

"What do you mean, they're not going to make it?"

"They won't be finished editing in time."

"But they told me this morning everything was fine!"

"Well, they say the editor was too slow."

"Why tell me this now? Why didn't they cut some fucking corners? Why has he told you just twenty minutes before fucking airtime? Mark, for Christ's sake! Can they rush whatever they've got to the feed point and send it live? We'll take it live, Mark! We don't have a choice!"

"No, John, that won't work. The film is a long way from being finished and the feed point is at least half an hour from where they are."

"Jesus fucking Christ!! You *never* miss your feed time! *Ever!*"

Except at Television New Zealand.

So, at 7:00 PM, two million screens in New Zealand went blank. Nothing. Then music, followed by an announcement over a TVNZ caption: "The advertised program will not be seen tonight. Here is a replacement program." It was one of the more memorable disasters in the history of New Zealand television.

The crack Flying Squad wanted an argument. No, it wasn't their fault. So they missed the deadline. So what? You're taking this too seriously, John. Besides, we do have great material and we've almost finished editing now. So why don't we run it on Wednesday? So Wednesday it was, two days' time, again at 7:00 PM.

The Flying Squad met the deadline this time. No hold-ups. No surprises. Well, just one. The documentary was dreadful. No drama, no emotion, little else but endless shots of yachts sailing up and down the western coast of Australia.

The Flying Squad flew no more. And I vowed never again to listen to New Zealanders, especially while urinating.

17

If Only You'd Been Shot

After the America's Cup disaster and a very public berating, I descended into mental hell. And became one of them, a Kiwi again. It wasn't difficult. Growing up in New Zealand, I was an eager participant in "the six o'clock swill," a nightly, male-only, one-hour orgy during which we forced down as much alcohol as we could until the pubs closed at six. We then sprayed the sidewalks with vomit before staggering off to meet the sheilas or going home to the wife. But I went one figurative step—or stagger—further this time. I also gulped down fistfuls of a narcotic prescribed by a Wellington psychiatrist. He was a man who tried to evoke the air of a great and infallible healer. He was wealthy and urbane. As I lay on his couch, he purred his approval of the stylish imported socks I had donned that morning. But what about the meds? Aren't fourteen pills an awful lot to be taking in one day? What about the toxicity level?

"No idea, old son. But can ask a pharmacist friend of mine, if you like. How about we meet again next week and I should have the answer. That'll be seventy dollars, please."

The pharmacist's verdict? I was taking a near-fatal dose and it might be a rather splendid idea if I stopped. Too late. I was addicted.

After two months in a psychiatric hospital in bleak and cold

Dunedin, on New Zealand's South Island, I figured Television New Zealand had beaten me. A Sunday newspaper found my hospitalization for depression and sleeping pill addiction newsworthy enough to run as a front-page story. That's when I decided it was time to leave and go back to Canada to rejoin the CBC. My first assignment? Beirut. Again.

On the way in to Lebanon, via Syria this time, we stopped in the lush Bekaa Valley for lunch. I remember having a plate of hummus with pita bread and a Pepsi. I also remember waking up on the floor of the Commodore Hotel that night, writhing as various fluids exited my body. I had not drunk the water at the restaurant, but I guess the glass had not been properly washed. Whatever, no Lomotil, Seef or sunshine was going to fix this leakage.

Around ten that night, a Red Crescent ambulance dodged artillery shells and grenades to get me to a Palestinian hospital in West Beirut. The diagnosis was easy: severe gastroenteritis. The cure, a wee bit more difficult.

"Oh, Mr. John, if only you'd have been shot. We would have you back on your feet in no time," lamented one of three doctors around my bed on the top floor, which had a sumptuous view of flashing artillery guns pounding the night away. "But we have no drugs for gastro. We've got lots of bandages and gauze and we really know how to treat gunshot wounds extremely well." He was almost blushing while I was still flushing.

"Mr. John, you'll have to go to Israel to get treated and you should do it very quickly."

"But I'm in a Palestinian hospital in West Beirut. How do I get to Israel from here?"

"Mr. John, Mr. John, do not worry. We have friends who will help you."

The doctors then wheeled me down to the basement and loaded me into another ambulance. The vehicle, which was marked with a red cross, took a secret route out of Beirut to an official Israeli border crossing. Not one soul asked any questions. I was offloaded into a private car and driven to a doctor's house in Jerusalem. I did not see any money change hands nor do I know what deal the Palestinians had with the Israelis. Sometimes even a journalist knows when to shut up and just be thankful for huge mercies.

It occurs to a giant brain like mine that, if those guys had the decency, courage, compassion and will to spirit one single, ailing journalist across a border and give him succor, why in the name of Allah and Abraham do they not help each other? Yes, yes, I know it is far more complex than that. Yes, there are factions, power struggles and outside influences. Yes, there is the history. Yes, the Wall and the settlements and impediments to peace. Yes, there is terrible poverty. And yes, suicide bombers kill innocent Jews, and Israelis assassinate Palestinians at will. But until the Palestinians, the Israelis and the United States start behaving like my ambulance drivers in Dushanbe or my doctors in West Beirut, the apocalypse will come. Not the one still merely dreamed of by the lunatic fringes of Christianity, Judaism and Islam, but an apocalypse where those lunatics run their very own asylum. And we will all be their victims.

18

What's the Why?

So why did I do it? Spend nine months a year away from home; risk getting killed; suffer terrible diseases; travel for months on end with folks whose sole aim in life was to out-fart and out-drink each other?

It all goes back to when I was a kid. I suffered from chronic, life-threatening asthma for the first fifteen years of my life. That meant less schooling than other kids, and when I was in class I was sometimes so drugged up on ephedrine, I had little idea of what was being taught. I failed exams with spectacular regularity with spectacularly low marks in everything but English. One school report said: "Despite his disability, John tries hard." That's as good as it got. At least until the New Zealand's National School Certificate Examination, in which, at the age of seventeen, I topped the entire country in English. My teacher, a priest, accused me of cheating. My parents thought it an aberration and advised me not to go to university to become a doctor as I'd wanted, but to settle into a trade; I'd be much happier doing that.

So my dad used his judicial influence with a court reporter and got me a job in the type-composing room of the local newspaper, *The Evening Post*. But the type room didn't want some weedy kid messing with their hot metal plates, so I was sent to the illustrations department. For a few months, all I did was file photos and throw out old printing blocks of the dearly departed. Then, one miraculous day, the illustrations editor, Charlie Cooper, actually let me write a caption for a photo that would be in tomorrow's paper. And I was hooked. One caption. One photo. The start of fifty years of journalism. First as a print reporter, then on to radio and finally television, where I have been for most of my life. Proving that the English exam wasn't a fluke.

I went to war zones because I was told to. That was the assignment. I've also been assigned to cover council meetings, mayors at rubber-chicken dinners, politicians talking nonsense during campaigns. I've also covered strikes, disasters, murders, oil spills, nuclear spills, illegal immigration, drunk driving, predator priests and a man who conversed with cabbages ... virtually anything that's happened, I've covered it. But each story I do with a passion and a conviction that is unshakeable. Journalists have an almost sacrosanct duty to get to the truth. Truth is what divides democracies from dictatorships. The many dangers inherent in the profession are, for me, just part of the job.

I never lusted after war zones. But they were always intriguing and very, very difficult to cover well. That was the attraction. I became very good at getting to the truth and finding the scenes that showed the truth in hellholes the world over. I have little fear but know when to be afraid. I am not easily intimidated and will not be frightened off a story by gunmen or bullies of any kind. I believe it is my duty to tell that story. If I don't, who will? Information and insight are what keep us socially alive and responsible citizens. Few people have the skills to bring the public that information and insight. When you have it, you must use it to the fullest of your abilities because it is a gift and a trust placed in you on behalf of your fellow humans.

I agree with the mantra that journalists should comfort the afflicted and afflict the comfortable, but I would go further. Journalists must have a sense of outrage at all the wrongs around them. And they must channel that outrage to reveal the wrongs so that all our lives might be better. A journalist must not tolerate half-truths and message tracks. It takes courage to challenge the president or the prime minister. That's the job. It takes courage to challenge the crooked CEO. That's the job. It takes courage to cover wars. That's the job.

Thank you for watching and please come back real soon. Then I can tell you the story about a man I know who sold an atomic bomb. True. But if any secret agents come a-knocking before I get a chance to finish the tale, don't fret. I'll hypnotize them with more war stories. I've got dozens of them.

About the Author

JOHN SCULLY was born in Westport, New Zealand. A childhood of asthma often cut months out of a school year. He never went to university and started work filing photographs at a Wellington newspaper and learned the dictionary from A–Z. That was his start in journalism. At twenty-four, he married Toni McCrea, and the next day, with his bride, left for London to join the British Broadcasting Corporation. He started as a summer-relief writer in the TV newsroom but soon rose to the position of duty editor. In 1974, Scully was recruited as the senior field producer for Canada's latest TV network, Global. He was courted by the U.S. networks but turned them down and remained in Canada to work for its other two major networks, CBC and CTV, for programs such as *The Journal*, *The National*, *the fifth estate* and *W-Five*. In his career, he has won numerous international awards for news and documentaries. He lives in Ontario with his wife and two cats.

Acknowledgments

I would like to thank my family for their amused tolerance. I am grateful to all the crews, reporters, editors, technicians and desk folks who helped me on the way. And a special thanks to the boys and girls who took all the happy snaps. They pissed me off then, because it meant we weren't shooting the story. Now I am in their debt. Damn.

Countries Worked In

Australia
Austria
Bahamas
Bahrain
Bangladesh
Barbados
Belarus
Belgium
Bosnia Herzegovina
Cambodia
Canada
Chile
China
Costa Rica
Croatia
Cuba
Cyprus
Denmark
Fiji
France
Germany
Great Britain
Greece
Grenada

Guyana
Honduras
Hong Kong
Hungary
India
Indonesia
Iran
Iraq
Ireland
Israel
Italy
Japan
Kenya
Latvia
Lebanon
Libya
Macedonia
Malaysia
Mali
Malta
Mexico
Morocco
Netherlands
New Zealand

Nicaragua
Northern Ireland
Pakistan
Palestine
Peru
Philippines
Russia
Scotland
Serbia
Singapore
South Africa
Sri Lanka
Switzerland
Syria
Tajikistan
Thailand
Uganda
Ukraine
Vatican City
Venezuela
Vietnam
Western Sahara
Zimbabwe

War Zones

Lebanon (13 times) 1978–1985
El Salvador (2) 1980, 1983
Israel–Lebanon–Gaza–West Bank
    (4) 1975–1995
Northern Ireland (11) 1968–1975
Nicaragua (2) 1981, 1983

Uganda (1) 1986
Vietnam (1) 1975
Sarajevo (1) 1995
Iraq–Iran (1) 1986